*A daughter's
memoir,
a writer's
journey home*

CIRCLE (*n.*)

CIRCLE (*n.*)

1a. ring, halo

5a. cycle, round
// the wheel has
come full
circle

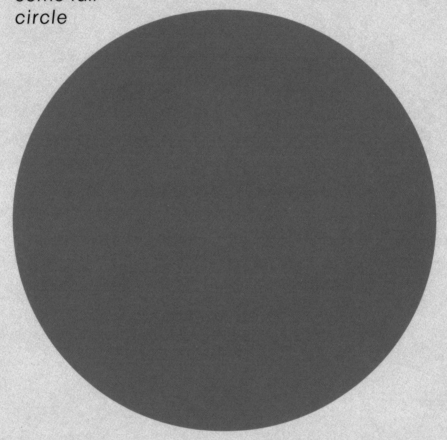

CIRCLE (n.)

1a. ring, halo

5a. cycle, round
// the wheel has
come full
circle

S W I R L (*v.*)

1a. to move with a whirling mass
or motion

1b. to pass
in whirling
confusion

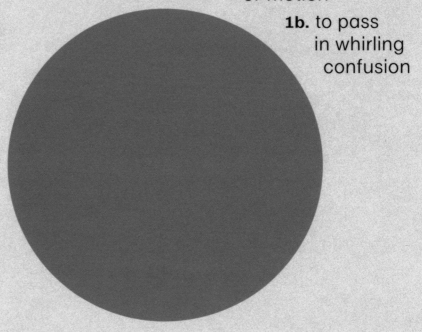

S W I R L (n.)

1a. to move with a whirling mass or motion

HURRICANE (*n.*)

1. a tropical cyclone with winds of 74 miles (119 kilometers) per hour or greater that occurs especially in the western Atlantic; usually accompanied by rain, thunder, and lightning

2. something resembling a hurricane, especially in its turmoil

HURRICANE (n.)

1. a tropical cyclone with winds of 74 miles (119 kilometers) per hour or greater that occurs especially in the western Atlantic; usually accompanied by rain, thunder, and lightning

2. something resembling a hurricane, especially in its turmoil

CIRCLE

WAY

CIRCLE

*A daughter's
memoir,
a writer's
journey home*

WAY

Mary Ann Hogan

WONDERWELL

The author's share of the proceeds from this book will be donated to the nonprofit Hogan-Newton Fund for young journalists at the Miami Foundation.

Library of Congress Control Number: 2021915373
ISBN 978-1-63756-012-9 (hardcover)
ISBN 978-1-63756-013-6 (EPUB)
Editors: Allison Serrell, Eric Newton
Author photo: Eric Newton
Cover design and interior design: Natalie Olsen
Cover illustration: *This Is How Thoughts Fly*, sketch by Bill Hogan
Inside cover illustration: *Winslow Homer Might Have Captured the Blue I Mentioned*, watercolor by Bill Hogan
Illustration opposite the title page: *Thoughts, Memories Exploding*, watercolor by Bill Hogan
Closing illustration, page 213: *Running Sea*, charcoal and pen sketch by Bill Hogan
The dictionary definitions are transcribed from *Merriam-Webster*

Published by Wonderwell in Los Angeles, CA
www.wonderwell.press

Distributed in the US by Publishers Group West and in Canada by Publishers Group Canada

Printed and bound in Canada

For William,
James, Annika,
Shade, Asher, and Haze,
who are writing the
next chapters.

≫ Untitled sketch, by Bill Hogan

Contents

"We are here to help each other get through this thing--whatever it is."

--Vonnegut

𝓦!ᵐ

⌃ Kurt Vonnegut quote, handwritten by Bill Hogan, from his notebooks
Bill's artistic signature, based on his full name, William

FOREWORD

Mary Ann Hogan wrote *Circle Way* over three decades, through good times and bad, as we raised our two sons in California, then Virginia and Florida, and finally back home again in the Golden State.

It started as the story of her enigmatic father, a prolific and influential literary critic haunted by the book he never wrote. Her search for the *why* of her father's story led back along his branch of the family tree and, eventually, deep into her own psyche.

Circle Way lives between journalism and poetry, weaving together the stories of

- great-great-grandfather **Patrick Michael Hogan**, the immigrant who flees the Irish potato famine to come to New York;
- great-grandfather **Hugh Hogan**, the lumber baron who builds much of the city of Oakland, yet dies penniless;
- great-uncle **Howard Hogan**, the wealthy Prohibition-era playboy whose prison sentence frees him;
- grandfather **Will Hogan**, the dapper Stanford man who wastes his life waiting for a fortune that never comes;
- father **Bill Hogan**, the writer who skips college to support his family yet wins a coveted job as book editor of the *San Francisco Chronicle*;
- and the author herself, **Mary Ann Hogan**, who pieces together her father's story—and in the doing, finds her own.

This book, Mary Ann would say, is about the people who escape the prisons of their own making and the people who don't.

⌃ Bill and Mary Ann Hogan, undated family photo

Abandoned by his father during the Great Depression, Bill Hogan made ends meet by becoming a journalist. Young Hogan's literary journalism caught the eye of soon-to-be-famous novelist William Saroyan. On January 9, 1936, Saroyan mailed Hogan a postcard, punched out on a manual typewriter, single-spaced, ending with this: "If you've got enough stories and sketches for a book, or a novel, will you tell me a little about it, and send the stuff to Bennett A. Cerf, Random House? My opinion is that he is the best publisher in America. With good wishes ..."

As it happened, there would be no book—not then, not ever: not after Bill Hogan became a well-regarded critic and a book offer came directly from publisher Cerf; not after Hogan had interviewed many of the nation's greatest writers; not even after he retired and the talk turned to a memoir.

Instead, Bill left behind notebooks full of vignettes, drawings, and paintings, as well as typewritten notes and scores of letters from the publishing world's elite.

To daughter Mary Ann, these artifacts showed how the stories of people's lives come to us in scattered bits, in fragments, and how it falls to every new generation to try to fill in the gaps, to feel whole, to bring it home.

Mary Ann braids into this book her father's art, most of it untitled, and his notebook entries, mixing in aged news clippings and slices of conversation, including an imagined rumor mill called *"talk of the town."* To all that, she adds musings on everything from a life-changing storm to the nature of nautilus shells, creativity, and truth.

Mary Ann hoped this book would speak to women who have unfinished business with their fathers; to mothers; to history lovers, thinkers, writers, and journalists; and to anyone feeling trapped, wondering what's really true, longing to get back to where they once belonged.

Like her father, Mary Ann Hogan was a journalist. She started this project as a straightforward journalistic memoir, but then started again as she earned her master of fine arts at Florida Atlantic University.

Circle Way became a quest "to fill in brackets, to find meaning where there was none"—to know not just her father, but herself, her own identity "as a fourth-generation Californian trying to survive in an alien landscape."

Mary Ann believed a traditional memoir would not respect the fragile sensibilities of memory. Often, she quoted writer Ben Yagoda: "Memory is by nature untrustworthy: contaminated not merely by gaps, but by distortions and fabrications that inevitably and blamelessly creep into it."

So, the book became a hybrid: part memoir, part lyric essay, part literary journalism, part traditional essay. Not an easy task. She had to commit what author Annie Dillard called an act of "creative courage ... you must demolish the work and start over." It took time and growth and a hurricane for Mary Ann to find that courage.

As a child, she was influenced by the writers her father championed. They echo here. *Circle Way* hops through time (Kurt Vonnegut) to tell the stories of those who came before (Alex Haley) with an infectious energy (Jack Kerouac), all the while feeling and revealing California (Joan Didion, John Steinbeck).

Mary Ann loved to teach—but she *had* to write. Had to sing the music of language to honor all she had read. Had to savor life a second time and, sometimes, had to keep her imagined barbarians just outside the gates.

In an earlier version of this manuscript, used as her master's thesis, she wrote: "I wanted this to be the book my father could never write, for whatever reason, for reasons that are somehow redeemed by the act of this writing."

Before Mary Ann could see her life's literary work published, before she could celebrate her escape from her own prison, she was forced to reopen a chapter of her life she thought was complete: that of lymphatic cancer.

We kept working on this book together in bed, the bed where my sons and I would hold her as she breathed her last.

◉

On February 14, 2019, four months before she died, my wife left a card on my nightstand. It asked, "Will you be my Valentine one more time and forever?"

The answer is in these pages.

Circle Way brims with valentines, and not the ones you might expect, such as her finishing her father's story and my writing the last chapter of hers.

There are valentines here to books and children and forgiveness and hope—but also there are melancholy Irish valentines, honoring a place where the author wasn't living and a father she couldn't understand—as well as tangled modern valentines of depression, anxiety, love, and courage so blended the makers of plastic-wrapped cards with red paper hearts have yet to fathom them.

———— Eric Newton ————

Mill Valley, California
AUGUST 15, 2021

My father, William Hogan, from 1955 to 1982 the literary editor of the *San Francisco Chronicle,* was a fulcrum for new talent, a champion of excellence. People knew him as a gentle soul who raised a happy family in beautiful, redwood-ringed Mill Valley, living a life many might envy.

John Steinbeck called him "an old and valued friend ... a man of taste and discernment."

Yet Bill Hogan, the influential book critic, a journalist who interviewed dozens of his century's seminal authors, a writer who published more than a million words—could not, would not, write a memoir.

In my father's notebooks, he sees himself as smaller than life, doubtful, vulnerable. He retreats into the third person, old school, more than humble, a journalist from the era when the reporter simply was not the story.

In so many ways, I am my father's daughter. Self-made journalists, we. Introverts, lovers of books and wine. Sufferers of "flying thoughts." We once held prized newspaper jobs, writing for the masses. But we felt like impostors with nothing to say. At times I still do.

My father, I believe, was emotionally crippled by the long reach of his once-famed anti-intellectual Catholic California family—devastated by its loss of fortune in the Crash of '29—a family that fell to pieces under the tyranny of its own prosperity.

Not too long after he retired from the *Chronicle*, I scrawled into my own clothbound journal:

> *I will write about my father. I will write*
> *about Uncle Howard. About the family*
> *that shaped them, about the people who*
> *escaped and the ones who didn't. About*
> *my dad . . . What it's like to be on the*
> *inside of what everyone won't talk about.*
> *I will write. I will write. I will write. . . .*
>
> *I will spend the rest of my life trying to*
> *fully know, fully understand, and fully*
> *appreciate what and who my father was.*

For decades, however, what I wrote about the book was that I couldn't write it—like my father before me, I am God of My Own Abyss, mired in a century of psychic debris.

> *I see myself sometimes as giving in to*
> *the impulse to retreat . . . to do what's*
> *comfortable, to go along with the program,*
> *put on appearances. I think that is what*
> *he did. My father regretted never having*
> *been A Writer . . .*
>
> *Can I do this?*
>
> *To what degree does family mean destiny?*

PROLOGUE

I discovered my father's notebooks tucked into the bookshelves of his backyard studio. Six clothbound volumes, pages once vacant, now covered in large block printing, drawings, paintings, sketches. Reading the entries, studying the images, feels like prying open a shell to find the unpolished gem inside, an accident of beauty. The result of some poor mollusk's fury to preserve himself, his haven invaded. A precious thing that began with an intruder, maybe small as a pebble, tiny as a grain of sand, maybe invisible, a mere molecule of pain, whose origins run just beyond the tide of knowing.

Blank Slate

I have never kept a journal (he recalls) Why? Maybe because the thoughts were not very good. Or important. The shaky spelling? The jokes? The under-mastery of language? Maybe time. No time for journals. Then, the embarrassment of a journal. Ego. Ergo, Ergot ... Take this book, [his wife] Phyllis said, on the next to the last day of his (my God!) seventy-fifth year. The seventy-fifth year in which he has not kept a journal. Someone (important, I am sure) once suggested I do a book called "Short Takes." Autobiography in vignettes.

Snatches. Snapshots. A record. Of what?—meetings, triumphs, lost opportunities, things I should have accomplished. Important (indeed) people. Sunrises, voyages, disgusts, funny stuff, pretentions. Short Takes, yes. But why?

Piecing together my father's story should help me see my own—*right?*—even if the gaps run deep. So why is this so hard? What is the source of my anxiety and depression? Does it swirl down the generations? I feel the need to fill in, to know where to fit, to look for my own accidents of beauty.

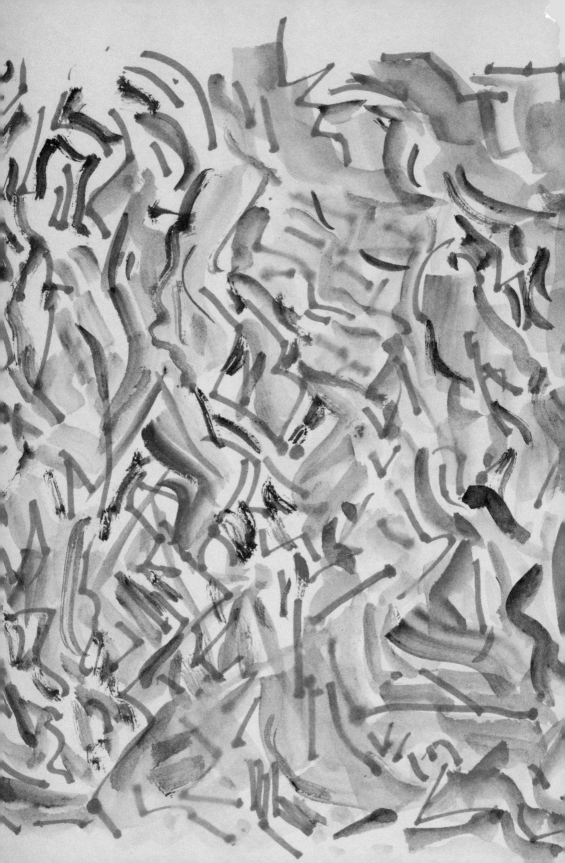

FRAGMENTS

I have lived, since the dawn of a new century, in this stretch of onetime swamp known as South Florida, a landscape I think of as *here*. Here, ghosts of dinosaurs dig into roadside canals. Birds in millinery finery flock overhead to land on foreign treetops. None of this would feel as strange were it not for the drumbeat of the seasonless sun. And for the guarded gate in front of my pastel terra-cotta suburban neighborhood, locking me into a place I never could have imagined living. And for the soil, where I try to grow tomatoes, grow anything, parsley, to help put things right.

Here, there is no soil to speak of, nothing deep brown, musty, life-giving. Just layers of white sand, eons-crushed rock and shell, marl. I dig a few inches down from the wilting tarragon, the shriveled tomatoes, and find fossils of sea creatures from half a million years ago, minuscule bits of houses of one crustacean or another, fragments from another geologic time.

Here, bananas grow, and mangoes.

There is a continent and lifetime away. A place of primeval redwoods; wild poppies like blankets on hillsides, jagged rocks and crushing waves sculpting coastal landscapes. Crabs tossed in steam pots in autumn. Fresh cream smothering cherries in summer. Wisdom-filled oaks whispering secrets in various kinds of weather. An occasional pumpkin vine or thistle of an artichoke dancing at certain sundown times. These things entered my marrow at birth as a fourth-generation Californian, the families of each of those generations working, living, struggling, all within thirty miles of one another, in and around San Francisco Bay.

We were never a clan for moving.

But I did.

Move.

And it fragmented me.

They are there, not here.

When I am here, not there.

Absent. Dependently claused, still, waiting.

Because of.

Here disquiets, discordant sunrises, indigestible smells. Surfaces strange to the touch, tepid and thorny beneath unsettled fingertips. Pulled-apart things. I remember as a child (it was *there*) a large dinner plate, a piece of Portuguese pottery, dropping from my hands onto my mother's cement floor. Shattered. We saw, felt, the shards, the broken of it. Some pieces large enough to glue back to a partial plate, a cracked Portuguese relic. Others, minuscule fractions, useless as an after-Christmas pine needle, or a stray eyelash.

⊙

Pieces of stories swirl around us, among, through. A Swedish scientist says the first germs of life on this planet may have been brought to Earth by "a fragment of an exploded world." Anthropologists digging in a gravel pit in England unearth the fragments of a human skull; experts judge it to be Paleolithic man. Excavators looking for a monument in a cemetery dig up a twenty-five-pound piece of a meteor composed of fused minerals, glass, stone and steel. A glass sliver from a broken automobile headlight leads to the arrest on manslaughter charges of a hit-and-run driver. Today: Partly cloudy, with low morning and evening fog, highs in the mid-60s.

A broken headlight. Chips from an ancient skull. A meteor in a cemetery. A weather report. An exploded world.

And then.

My life broke, like the Portuguese plate. I stopped writing. The words I needed to tell this or any story got locked away in some chest a thousand fathoms deep, soul disconnected from body. Days became a gray-dark hover, telling me I would never get home. When I finally pushed my periscope above water, it spied only enemy ships moving slow, creeping toward the pieces of me.

⊙

Songs of the ancient Greek poet Sappho, once perfect, harmonic, and whole, drift down to us only as fragments, slices of
verse, slivers of meaning. In her translation of Sappho, Anne
Carson uses brackets—] [—to mark missing-ness, inviting us
to imagine what could be.

Thus, one Sappho fragment reads:

so
]

]
]
]
]

Go   [
so we may see [
]
lady

of gold arms [
]
]
doom
]

I study this nautilus of a poem, its infinite twists and mysteries,
and wonder how different my life might be had I stayed *there*,
whether fewer brackets might inhabit my broken verse.

The quiet dust of my forebears feeds the California sod. Some of them I knew. Others, never. Still, their lives, quirks, desires, the logs they felled, the houses they built, their hardships, the prisons, real or imagined—these things still stir in me, particles of an inheritance. I try to cobble the distant pieces into something that might inform who I am here. This scattered attempt to know them grounds me, somehow, connects me to the soil they once walked upon, as I once walked. But I am not there. And suddenly they are all gone. I am an orphan many times over in a place that is not my own.

If I were Sappho:

]

then

[

now

maybe [[

[

[

because of

[

[

Answers

]

For the stories of the ones I never knew, I depend on the fractured memory of those who did, at least, when they were alive enough to remember. This, along with pieces of cracked china, a few time-eaten books, albums of crumbling news clippings from a wedding, an obituary folded into the back pages of a coverless Bible.

I start filling in brackets, connecting dots. Maybe that's what we do. A scientist friend tells me the Hubble Space Telescope proved that we have only a fragment of the universe in our grasp.

◎

"Daddy, are you feeling okay?"

"Wha … ?"

I spoke more slowly into the phone.

"Food. Are you eating?"

"Oh … well … you know … hospital food."

"And antibiotics? Are they giving you any?"

"Wha … ?"

Okay.

"Daddy?"

"Yes, Honey?"

"I love you."

"I know."

◎

I often imagine what my father would have said had he known that starting in the year 2001 I would be living here, in Florida, rather than there, place of his birth, of his mother's, of mine, my brother's. The place nobody in four generations of family ever left, not once since the day they settled and started building there, more than a century ago now, since my

Melancholy

FROM MY FATHER'S NOTEBOOKS

The first white blossoms of February begin to appear.
One more spring. My old friend Tom Cox's ashes lie under
a sycamore tree in their garden. He didn't see the blossoms
this year. He didn't get to finish the story. The mornings
are fresh, promising when I go out for the newspaper,
the Daily Woe. The blossoms bud, the bees still buzz in
the rosemary after a human life goes, the woe continues.
The melancholy seems to rise in me in the Afternoon . . .
but then, it always has (the inter-urban train in the
distance). The promising blue-bright morning is a haze
by 4 p.m. Then the night comes.

great-grandfather Hugh, a rugged and rich West Coast lumber baron, sliced down half the trees in Northern California to build up the city of Oakland.

I can almost hear my father's voice, kind but wry, tentative, always just a puff and a worry away from some imagined hurt. He would inhale a cigarette deep into his caving chest, sigh, then physically melt further inward, his torso slightly crumpling into gentle concavity, his hands moving to his belly, as if protecting himself from some unexpected force of nature.

"Oh, my aching back" was the phrase my father used for whatever served the dislocated moment. Something from the newspaper that riled or dispirited him. The odd piece of unexpected news. A marital breakup, a dredged swamp, a neighborhood cat lost, a eucalyptus tree chopped to the nub. Or maybe one of his children announcing they were going out to dinner forty miles away. Even moving across the bay to his boyhood home of Oakland. ("Oakland, for God's sake. Oh, my aching back!")

Or Florida.

"My God! Nobody ever went to Florida!" I'm sure he would have said. "Except maybe that faker Spaniard—what's his name? Ponce de León. Of course. The Fountain of Youth, for God's sake."

Over the years, I made it my job to soothe those moments, to make him upright again, even for a short time, a minute, two, three, pumping helium back into a balloon with a slow but steady leak.

"But, Daddy," I would have said, trying to ease the distress. "There are things you would love about Florida. Sunken ships off the coral reefs, the mystery of the reefs themselves." I would have told him about the Everglades naturalist Marjory Stoneman Douglas, who called Florida "a country that the sea has conquered and has never left." But I know it wouldn't have mattered, wouldn't have soothed. Because when Stoneman Douglas says "the sea," she means the Atlantic, which is not the Pacific, which is part of the trouble I'm having trying to live here, which is why I hear my father's voice saying, *"Florida?!"*

The Pacific is my father's ocean.

The Pacific is wild, in my breath and his, in our bones, in the bones of those who came before us. Ships crossed in fog there and sometimes wrecked on rocks just below the surface. Visitors marveled at how that ocean fed into a huge bay through a relatively small mouth.

Seeing it, soldier-explorer John C. Frémont recalled the Golden Horn of the Bosporus in the capital city of empires past, Constantinople. He named the strait the Golden Gate.

In summer and autumn, the northern hills above the strait, the dry-grain hills, burn gold with sun.

◎

Strange about the fury of that ocean. *Pacific* means "peaceful."

My father loved that ocean, the ships that crossed there, the freighters that went there, sometimes ghosts through the fog, other times, shoulder-squared, straight-nosed freighters hell-bent on Shanghai, "proper freighters," as my father would say. He read about them, kept files on them, collected books about them. He wrote about them and sketched them in his private notebooks. He dreamed of one day writing his own books about them.

◎

Lost Ships

FROM MY FATHER'S NOTEBOOKS

I tried to do a book about "ship watching"—how to identify by stack-flag profiles, design, etc., in the 1960s. I gathered a mass of photos. But things changed so rapidly. Containers, mostly—that the book never worked out. Some of those pre-container freighters and pre-cruise ship lines were beauties. No book, it turns out. But not a bad hobby. I wonder if somehow along the line I managed a drop of Brendan the Navigator in me.

One notebook entry he titled: "Books That Never Got Written."

Things on my father's desk in the clapboard artist studio where he worked behind our house:

- Sutliff pipe tobacco.
- *Columbia Encyclopedia.*
- Silver letter opener shaped at its end like a schooner.
- Toy monkey (yellow vest, pipe in mouth) on the windowsill, with the label, typed in bold capital letters and pinned to the toy monkey's chest: WRITER.

The notebooks he kept to himself. But I know he meant them for me. Those last few years of his life he spent hours each day in his backyard artist studio, reading, combing the encyclopedia ("My *real* education," he called it), digging up facts about popes or Mesopotamia, cats or Siberian winters, the habits of hedgehogs, shipwrecks and weeds. He drew, painted, wrote down his stories, sometimes in shaky letters, about his decades as literary critic for a powerful West Coast newspaper; about the war, when he was an editor on the US Army newspaper, the *Stars and Stripes*; about his family, the parents, grandparents, the people who seared him, stifled him. He rarely talked about them but spent much of his life struggling to escape their grasp.

His writings are not so much stories as sketches, fragments of a life haphazardly stitched into patches, pen, ink, pastels, graphite, the pricking needle telling him time was running low. He wrote snippets about his garden, the worms he dug for his pet chicken, hopes for his children, the driftwood he hunted,

Ulysses at Times

FROM MY FATHER'S NOTEBOOKS

If you could take one day, any day—50 years ago, 30—and reconstruct it, what would you find? Impossible, of course, though Joyce tried it in "Ulysses." I wonder how many people have read "Ulysses." Not me. Sections and in and around. Or Finnegans Wake (never with the apostrophe). Difficult stuff. You could take parts of days, maybe. Then add them altogether? Even then ... An April morning with flawless Blue Sky. The theater of that Midnight Mass at St. Peter's in Rome, Christmas Eve, 1944. The Blue of the Sea of Oregon from the low main deck of the lumber ship at 5 a.m. in July. Not even the Med. or the Sea of Cortez was that blue. Well, maybe. But it wasn't that undulating Blue, the swells. Yes, but you were 16 or 17 then. It's like the taste of peaches—it's never the same when you're older. Isn't that right, Stephen Dedalus?

friends he missed, the authors he had known, interviewed, written about: Steinbeck, Haley, Didion, Vonnegut, Capote, too many to name in a pass. He knew that one day I would find the notebooks, maybe pull them into—what? A poem? A book? A series of articles? Something that he never did, maybe never could. Why? I still don't know. Then again, maybe he never meant for them to see daylight. Maybe I am invading his shell. *Daddy, tell me what to do.*

What I do know: the notebooks were his private harbor, a place to unload the freighter of his imagination, a deep-water ship, trolling ideas that charmed or haunted him, like the wonder in a piece of literature discovered ("Hawthorne! After all these years!"); the accidental beauty of a spider's web; the myriad colors of blue; the poetry he heard in a cargo manifest from the day's shipping news—cargo from Mombasa, Kenya: cinnamon, 337 bags; elephant tusks, ten cases; blue poppy seeds, 520 bags.

I struggle to fill in the brackets, to find the answer to the puzzle that was my father.

HERE

I have come to believe that *here* is more an idea than a place, a dislocation of psyche, not a particular corner of Earth. *Here*, in the plain sense, could be Florida, or Virginia, as it has been for me, or for that matter, it could be the veldt of South Africa. The feeling of *here* lies, not in the kinds of trees you encounter, the smell of a sky or a season, but rather, in the absence of *there*—the heart of *here* being elsewhere. I think of the California coastal redwoods, towering spirits whose shallow root systems protect them from harm. The roots reach four to six feet deep, but spread out underground as far as 125 feet, roughly thirty human arms, shoulder to fingertip, fingertip to shoulder, reaching out in all directions. The pilgrim roots meet those of the tree next to them, the one next to that, and the next, an interlaced family, binding generations, holding one another in place. For me, no matter where *here* happens to be, those root links are gone.

Palm Beach County, Florida, 2005, the afternoon before the hurricane

We came here four years ago for my husband's job, for a future with fine schools and orange trees, the upgrowing of it all, boundless promise. And right now, we are waiting, watching, listening, glued to the Florida television stations, changing channels, looking for anything new, a shred of news, a sign.

> *The speed of this storm is now, has now increased, with winds more than 115 per hour, as Wilma strengthens.*

Channel change.

> *We are tracking Hurricane Wilma, here at the four o' clock hour, Dan, and it looks like Wilma is heading straight for South Florida.*

We are not eating, not talking. Not praying, at least not yet, who knows why.

> *That's right, Angela. Governor Bush has made it very clear that this is a serious*

storm, and many Floridians, some people
here, are still in denial about the power of
this thing.

My sons, ages twelve and almost sixteen, have brought in the mat and sidings from our backyard trampoline, shaken all the coconuts they could from the palms and stashed them in the garage in buckets. In Florida, you learn that flying coconuts, flying anything, can smash windows, yours, your neighbor's, and if windows smash, a house can implode. We have just gone through the ritual of stocking pantry and garage with bottled water, cans of tuna, a first-aid kit, cat food, can openers, hydrogen peroxide, pounds and pounds of coffee, finely ground, for when we lose electricity and have to make coffee on the five-hundred-pound barbecue out back.

In my earnest efforts to try to make peace with where I live, I have learned that this tropical pocket of earth is the ancestral home of the Taíno, the Native Caribbeans who centuries ago pounded on drums and danced to a fury to ward off the hurricanes conjured by the fierce goddess Guabancex. Life is knit deep into the myth of creation in this whirling region of mangoes and shipwrecks and sun. My father would have loved that story, the story of the wonder of natural things, of how the Mayans too had a deity, Huracán, the god of wind, storm, and fire.

More than anything, my father would have loved the art, the images, sculptures and water jugs, creations of the Taíno, their roaring deity, with cyclonic spirals for arms, swirls round a body or a head. We would have talked about how the people from so long ago could have known, from their humble perch just feet above the mud, that the storms their gods brought were spiral shaped, vortices.

"Imagine that," I can hear my father saying. "Those poor little people—well, maybe they weren't so poor or little—were so smart they figured it out without modern science—meteorological radar, or whatever it was we had after the war. An ancient mystery. A marvelous mystery. Of art, of human nature."

How *did* they know?

"They knew," my father would have said, "because they had eyes and ears and were smarter than You Know Who." This, meaning the Catholic God of his childhood, the tribune deity that his family—mother, grandparents, aunts—shrouded themselves in, used to barricade themselves against the world of ideas, of intellect, a world my father was drawn to, even at age thirteen, when Father Lacy, his Latin laced with Irish brogue, made him an altar boy.

My father was charmed by the idea of deities of other cultures. The Old Testament god Yahweh in his infinite wrath. The hamadryads of Greek legend, who lived in and protected the trees. And maybe his favorite, Thoth, the Egyptian god of scribes, said to have brought himself into being through the power of language. Thoth was in charge of libraries and all things written.

"My kind of god," my father would say. "A proper god."

He was not opposed to deity. Only dogma.

I know he would have loved the Caribbean gods of life and death, creation and destruction, would have sketched them in his notebooks, the swirling arms, the vortical body, drawings to which, I am sure, he would have added the caption: "Yahweh, or Someone, is in charge (I hope)."

First Mass

He was scared—like an actor in his first part. An early mass when few people are there. My mother, of course, was there watching, watching little Billy in surplice and cassock, fresh, going through the motions, not really believing, ringing the little bell, lighting the candles, the candelabra something chipped off a Sicilian Cathedral, I think. Later the grandmother and the aunts came. "He'll be a priest!" said the grandmother. "Thanks be to God!" my mother said. But God had other plans. Always did. Always will. (Thank you, God.)

We are beating our own drums, lighting our own fires. We have cleaned out a closet in the middle of the house, stocked it with water, pillows, cereal bars, more cat food, bleak essentials, it seems, for lives that in sixteen or so hours will surely be whipped to shreds. We have brought in two garden hoses, a broken shovel, potted plants, even dead ones, tomato cages, remnants of a garden that never seems to grow.

I have carried in the treasures from my parents' California garden, things I have always cherished, now in my Florida backyard. The pelicans, three ceramic, two cast-iron, one wood. My parents believed pelicans were mystical. Maybe because they survived the extinction scare of the 1970s. My mother and father would spend hours at the driftwood beach watching their prehistoric forms dip in and out of the surf, lines of eight, ten pelicans at a time moving in harmonic rhythm, in, out, barely skimming the waves, their line now breaking off into two, three, then two again, that pair drifting off, connected at wing tip, up from the ocean and over the cliffs.

A statue of a puppy, a gray stone likeness of their pet beagle, Murphy, who tagged along on their weekend trips to the beach. Murphy always escaped her leash, galloping down the rough pebbled sand, unfettered, chasing seagulls, sometimes finding a dead one, rolling in it, front to back, back to front, reveling in the gorgeously rotting smell of dead bird.

My father's collection of shells, including two nautilus he found on a beach in Mexico the time he journeyed to Baja, California, to deliver boxes of books to a bookless library.

His rotting buoy, salvaged from the driftwood beach, loosed from some barge, or maybe from a spunky tug guiding a tanker to port. "Who knows what this buoy has seen," he said as he nailed it to his backyard fence. "Japan, maybe. Australia. Think of it."

Pieces of driftwood he found as he scoured the beach for firewood, too beautiful to burn, nature's knotty, sea-twisted art, part of the backyard gallery of my inheritance.

Here began eleven years ago, when my husband found his first dream job on the Atlantic Coast. I remember the day, the smell of the sky, a smoky California fall.

"What would you do if we moved to Virginia?" my husband said.

"I'd probably start smoking again."

"Virginia, the Tobacco State," he said in a nervous laugh. "You can probably still smoke in restaurants there. They probably encourage it."

I had been a nonsmoker for—how many years? But just the hint of the word *Virginia* made me want to smoke.

"What do you mean, 'if we moved to Virginia'?"

"Well, there's a job—an unbelievable job. You know how we always talked about, someday there'd be a job we couldn't turn down?"

Did we talk about jobs?

Did we say they would be in Virginia?

That they would be anywhere else other than California?

I had visited the East Coast many times, love New York, Washington, Maine. But visiting is visiting. Not ripping a native plant from its soil. The only thing I knew about Virginia was its place as the seat of the Confederacy, a place where people died defending their right to own African slaves, where early colonists named a spot Jamestown after the Stuart king who first ordered the Holy Bible translated into English. I knew Virginia got rich growing tobacco, and maybe they grew it still, and that was fine with me, because all I wanted to do was smoke.

And figure out a way to tell my father.

My mother was the strong one, the realist, the one who could soothe by reminding me of her own great-grandmother who had to leave Norway to come to California with nothing but a copper pot and a trunk full of clothes, and who survived. My mother could find a way to make anything, even moving across the country, seem exciting. My father saw only the gray dark. I spent a good part of my life trying to bring him glimmers of what passed for happiness, the crooked half smile when I told him a funny story, brought him a newspaper article I'd written, delivered to him two fine grandsons. He would wither, I was sure, without my constant efforts to keep him afloat. It was after dinner.

We sat in front of the massive brick fireplace, the fire fed by my father's weekly haul of driftwood.

"We'll be just outside of Washington—just thirty minutes away from the White House," I said. "And all the museums. You and Mom can come to visit. And I'll bring the boys back every summer." No change in his face. He stared straight on, fixed on some point in space just beyond my right shoulder. "We can watch the leaves turn in the fall. I know you'll love that. We'll go to the Smithsonian, watch the leaves."

My father would sometimes get a look on his face, a look that said he was no longer hearing. He had retreated, the hermit crab back to the whelk, scanning the insides of things, searching his private storehouse of thoughts, images from a past or a daydream, something that, when he surfaced, would help bring into focus what he could not put into words. "The Narrative" is the name my father had for the place where he stored odd things, the quirky event, the unplanned encounter, passing thoughts and fancies, hurts, lines from *New Yorker* cartoons, scenes from trips, memories of ships, things that mattered, all stored away into his imaginary repository, the Narrative, uppercase *N*. These disparate contents, chewed by time, just might add up to a life, but then, they might not. There was the catch. As he always said, you could never understand it all, could never make sense of the design, if there was one, while it was still in motion. He said it was like an ant trying to follow the lines of a Persian rug.

Like a lot of writers, I suppose, my father fantasized about being able to trick the Narrative at its own game. *I just hope I live long enough to see how it all comes out*, he often thought, often said. *I just want to see how it all comes out.*

"Virginia!" he finally said. "Well."

Long pause. "Think of it. An adventure."

Did I ever see him cry? Not that I remember. At least not tears. His tears spilled inward, I think, where they pooled somewhere deep, turning solid, then smoldering, growing tentacles that pulled at his insides, shriveling his frame a bit more.

He stood up, turned around, slow, and walked out the sliding glass door, across the back patio to his studio, where he lay down on the single bed that served as his office sofa and his spot for daily naps. He would sleep now, escape the pain.

In his notebooks my father painted a picture of a rounded blue-green vessel of some kind, a vase, a bowl, blurs of flags and flowers spewing up and out into the air. The caption:

> *Container of Souls ready to be used.*
> *Or recycled Souls.*
> *Or rejected Souls . . . Take your pick.*

Container of Souls Ready to Be Used,
or Recycled Souls, or Rejected Souls —.
- - Take your pick.

≳ *Container of Souls*, watercolor, from my father's notebooks

I remember the orange truck, almost half a block long, pulling alongside our tiny blue Edwardian-era house in Oakland. It took them eight hours to wrap and stack the plates, chairs, toys, books, phonograph records, unopened birthday candles, a sparrow's nest we'd found in the holly bush, shards of lives stashed in a truck bound for someplace other than home. Among the books was the cracked leather-bound album of brittle newspaper clippings describing the teas, luncheons, and garden parties leading up to the storied 1911 wedding of my father's parents—grandmother Mildred, society belle, to my grandfather Will, elder son of the Oakland lumber baron Hugh Hogan. I often imagined that our little blue Edwardian house, with cupola, winding mahogany stair rail, elaborately carved front door, was the work of Old Man Hugh himself. Could have been.

I stood in front of the house with my two small children, ages four and almost one, as the huge orange truck pulled away. My youngest was christened there in that house with the cupola, a place just half a mile from my father's childhood home. My husband was already in Virginia, working late, hard, as always. I remember thinking, we're not so much going to one place as we are leaving the other. We're taking the things we own but leaving leafy back roads, pathways through neighbors' yards, the things that made us. Friends, children of friends, people you could call on if something went wrong. Four generations of family, acres of landscape in my blood, sculpting me, like the Mendocino River rocks in my front yard, rocks I'd scavenged from the creek at my brother's farm, an armful each summer, once crags on a mountain now polished smooth as moons by eons of cradling California water.

◎

Soon after the move to Virginia, I slipped on the green shag carpet covering the staircase leading up to the bedrooms. Slid at the top of the stairs. Went down on my tail, right leg first. *Where was the left?* I don't remember the fall so much as the scream, a roar, low, someone else's voice: "Oh my God my bones are crunching I hate living here please take me home." Each step down came a crack, the ankle, the leg, bone snapping like maple limbs in a freeze, thoughts coming at me, stairs coming at me, worlds going somewhere, bones elsewhere, bone smashing on bone, a three-second journey that felt like an hour, a lifetime.

My husband kneeled over me *oh God*.

He called an ambulance.

The lady on the phone wanted to know how many stairs. Four? Ten?

Light starch? Heavy?

My husband cradled my right foot in his arms, holding it in place. "Don't look at the foot," he said. I looked at the foot. It didn't look like a foot. It looked like the hairless head of a grotesquely misshapen newborn baby, sticking out ninety degrees from my leg.

"Please don't look," he said again.

I looked.

I passed out.

⌾

A shattered ankle meant three months in a wheelchair, more than a year and a half walking with a cane. Because of the seven or more pieces of bone pinned together with steel plates and screws, we had to hire a babysitter to keep my one-year-old son from crawling up on my lap, from snuggling with his mommy, all he wanted to do, all I wanted to do, but he might disturb the slowly healing bones, so he couldn't. Because of the ankle, I couldn't take my sons back to California that summer to visit my mother and father, their grandparents. To visit them so my sons could know the place of my childhood, the massive brick fireplace, the backyard haven of a garden with daphne bush, Japanese plum, poppy patch, rhododendron hedges swallowing the back fence, the secret path bathed in wandering blackberry leading up to the neighbor's yard; a view of the stately mountain just beyond reach, where fog tumbled down those summers, turning Fourths of July to a damp, soupy chill that we gamely greeted with sparklers.

Because I could not take my sons back to California that summer to play in the garden, I never saw my father again.

"Daddy," I said over the phone, from my screened back porch in Virginia. It was snowing. I was out on the porch, smoking. My children slept.

"Yes, honey?" He was in Kaiser Permanente hospital in San Rafael, California, with pneumonia, hard time hearing, breathing, understanding, waiting on time.

"I love you," I said.

"I know," he said, a rasp.

The next morning, he was gone.

When he died, I thought of things that move and things that don't. What moves: cattle or ants heading home; soft ripples of air, of sand dunes, of breath; stones skimming, skipping, slicing on mirrors of water, anything swelling like water, the tide; jump starts, hand slaps, the tremble as he walked with his cane;

Falling

FROM MY FATHER'S NOTEBOOKS

Autumn in Winter. It is winter here, moving toward February. I saw the first hint of Blossoms in the Japanese plum yesterday. Cold, but they don't care. Pretty soon the white blossoms. An old pop song: "Spring Will Be a Little Late This Year." An old Robert Nathan title: "One More Spring." But I think of Autumn. Or that American word, Fall.

Dropping.

Descending (the dictionary says).

The season when leaves fall, Autumn. Sometimes when I read the obit pages I feel like one of the last clinging leaves.

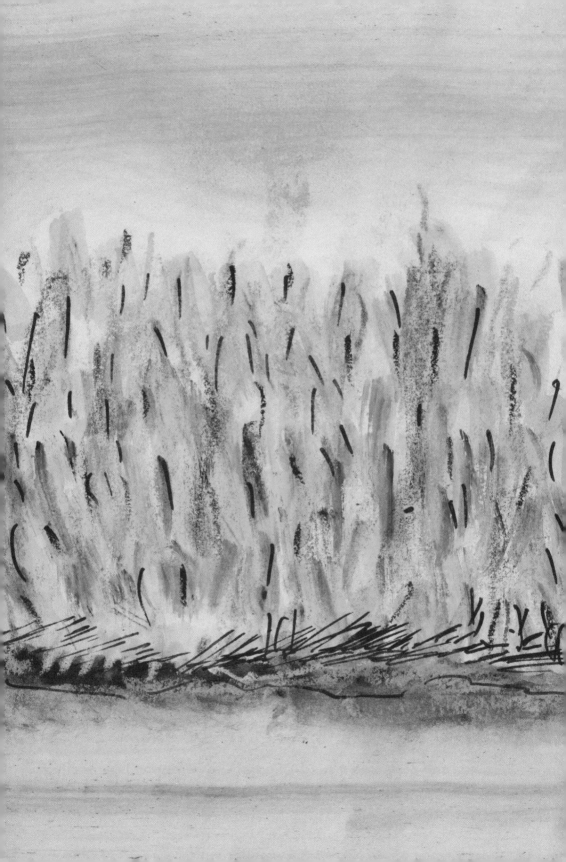

his black-rimmed glasses flecked with white, slipping down his unsuspecting nose.

What doesn't: boulders, lampposts, fossils, diamonds, sunken ships; ducks as they stand in a pummel of rain, marshaled to duty, spit shined, oiled, safe. The expanse of skin where my father once lived, an ash-white terrain, no shimmer, just smooth, no flecks of dandruff, no red scaly skin at the ears, no saggy jowls; no black-rimmed glasses with snow dustings, no breath. Just an oversized quiet, no home, no going, an empty nautilus shell, yawning wide.

Palm Beach County, Florida, 2005, the night before the storm

Maybe we should be praying now. To Yahweh, to the Egyptian god Thoth, to the Caribbean god of the swirling arms, to any god kind enough to hear us. The minutes tick. We wait. Listen, we have no one to pray to. The TV is talking.

> *We are in the final hours now, with*
> *Wilma moving northeast, at eighteen*
> *miles per hour, winds now at 125, and*
> *expected to increase, as Wilma heads*
> *directly toward Palm Beach County.*

Cut to news clip of a Key West resident:

> *They're telling me to get out. This is*
> *my home. The only home I know.*
> *They can't make me leave—can they?*

THERE

There is the place I was born to, a landscape as present as breath. Strange, you don't dwell on colors, the curve of earth, the sounds of the place you spring from, just as you don't think about breath, the in and out, the rise and fall, being. But then something shifts. The earth tilts. The sun slants. A tree dips. The breath stops, for a second. And then, as if for the first time ever, you see, with preternatural clarity, the place that cradled you, even when you weren't looking. Even something as small as a hermit crab scrabbling to claim a home in someone else's shell. Foghorns at night, aching sad brays, miles of pushing and reaching through the dense wet, a sound of distant longing. Or the poppies, a burst on a hill by a roadside, a riot of velvet in orange; waves of orange petals, the velvet underside of orange, not the orange of parades, but of unforeseen moonrise. I can see the driftwood—the feel of my father—the knotty, twisted shards and shapes from a tree or an unbuckled ship, tumbling down rivers, bouncing on rocks down rivers, finding their way to the ocean, tossed again and again to the shore.

Then come the hayfields of Sonoma County, where my brother and I spent summers of our childhood, wide, waving acres of gold, oceans of sweet, warm, wet, a summer of smells; a wooden barn in graceful disrepair; cud-chewing cows eyeing the wideness, the hay splashing up hillsides, swimming up and over the low white and gold hills framing the valley that held the barn where we swung over bales of hay, smelled the unforgiving sweet of the hay.

The ocean, always the ocean, a place of deep longing, haunted secrets, fiercely loved by seekers of violence, of passion, a place of roaring, cradling, crashing, smoldering; an untamed place of murmurs, rocks and shoals; a place of rupture, surfaces breaking, laughing, of rock jutting up to kiss the surface, a place where just below, formless jellyfish, clams, and whelk skip along with the drift, a drifting place, and above, seabirds glide through tangles of white caps, white sharpness, all of it in me churning, mostly by night.

Woodhooking

FROM MY FATHER'S NOTEBOOKS

My firewood is getting low again in this cold winter.
I buy it now, and that distresses me. For decades I
scrounged firewood, beaches, building sites ... It was a
game. A treasure hunt. Driftwood and good building
scrap coming down from the rivers. One year a barge
came loose from a tug off Cronkite and smashed onto
the rocks, littering the beach with—firewood! A bonanza
for weeks! We haven't been there in months, it seems.
Difficulty walking. Time running out. I wonder who will
hook the driftwood after I'm gone?

St. Mary Cemetery, Oakland, California, thirty years earlier

How to account for the absence of angels?

The Old Man didn't have a one. Strange, as angels were all around him. Weeping cherubs, life-size forms and larger, as angel stature goes; stony-robed emissaries, fingers pressed in prayer, heads cocked up toward some airy path connecting the here of the graveyard to a there of something better. Each was dearly paid for, placed by wife, child, or friend, or perhaps a favorite nephew. Even a group of brethren from one secret society or another. Clearly, someone, at some time, wanted it known down the ages that one grand life or another once walked on this green earth.

The Old Man, my great-grandfather Hugh, barely got a whisper. Just a plaque in the ground, no bigger than a brick nearly covered by turf, King Richard ii's "little little grave" inscribed with just one word, the family name: Hogan.

A handful of the shrinking Hogan clan, my father among us, gathered in 1984 on a Sunday to set it right. At least a little right. A distant cousin and I had purchased a real headstone, made of granite, Impala Black granite with polished top and rough sides, to mark the place where the Old Man lay. I am still not quite sure why. A bow to a pull of the soil? Some ancestral finger beckoning, inviting us to carry out our own version of water and oil libations offered to generations past? I once read that our ancestors "dwell in the attics of our brains," that they inhabit our cells. Beings, phantoms, cellular memories, you can try to ignore them, but you can't escape them.

The headstone was my cousin's idea. It was only right, he said, the least we could do to honor the patriarch who came West to start it all. Old Man Hugh, the old-sod scrapper who left Buffalo by cargo vessel in the 1880s with just pennies, then built a lumber empire, then built half a city, then got richer than Gilgamesh, then was so pleased with his turns of fate that on Sundays, according to my father, he jangled his silver dollars into the collection plate at St. Leo's Catholic Church so everyone could hear the music of his bounty.

His army of choppers and sawyers and splitters turned Humboldt redwood and Puget Sound pine into millions and millions of board feet of lumber, timber sliced from the forests, rent from towering spirits of the Northern California coast, lumber to build up a city, a waterfront, a monument to live on, an expanse of a prize to take the place of the angel that no one, not one of his children, thought to place at his grave.

Searching through old newspaper archives, where the ghosts lay, I could trace at least an outline of the Old Man's life, his travels. Officer in the Knights of Columbus. Pillar of St. Leo the Great Catholic Church, booster of civic causes, owner of fine automobiles and mostly obedient children. Also builder, much of it with his own hands, of a Stick-Eastlake Italianate Victorian mansion on a hill in Oakland, a player piano inside, and a carved front door with filigree-laden brass door knocker he bought one time in Florence. He attended white-tie business banquets. He gave speeches to civic men about the great good fortunes of his lumber company, the largest on San Francisco Bay. He talked about how proud he was, how honored, to be able to tie that great good fortune to the greater fortune of the city of Oakland, California, just beyond the reach of the fog belt, two miles across the bay from San Francisco, the gold-rush boomtown that Conan Doyle called the "floating vice of the Pacific." Oakland was different. Oakland was sturdy, steadfast, like the Old Man himself.

A story on the front page of the *Oakland Tribune*, May 15, 1944, headlined "Funeral Held for Pioneer," included only the barest facts of his life, plucked here:

> *Oakland lumberman and capitalist*
> *Died Saturday*
> *Requiem high mass held*
> *Interment at St. Mary's Cemetery*
> *Co-founder of Hogan Lumber Company, 1888*
> *Owned many properties, including wharf*
> *property below Alice Street*
> *Hogan Lumber Co. oldest in Oakland*
> *Survived by . . .*

Old Man Hugh was survived by four of his eight children. From my childhood, I knew of just two. Will Hogan, my grandfather, whom I loved beyond telling those early years, who gave me a crinoline petticoat one year for Christmas, I must have been five, who told me and my brother stories and read us books. Also, Howard Hogan, the surprise baby bouncing around the Victorian mansion, Old Man Hugh's "mistake," my father often said. Howard, the great-uncle who died well before I was born but about whom I had heard stories, since I was a little girl, from my grandfather Will.

Survivors, but no angels. Hundreds of brackets to fill.

I read through the cracked black leather wedding album my grandmother Mildred kept for half a century in her cedar chest, the album I brought with me from California to Virginia to Florida. It holds dozens of yellowed newspaper stories chronicling Mildred's elaborate wedding to my grandfather Will, the Old Man's oldest son. St. Joseph Catholic Church in Alameda. Three hundred guests in fashionable assemblage. Breathless newspaper accounts of the bride's dress, an imported robe of pearl satin; an overdress of chiffon embroidered in pearls and tiny silk orange blossoms; a long double panel of rose point falling from bodice top to train, where it was caught with a garland of orange blossoms. The mother of the groom, Anastasia, wife of Old Man Hugh, wore a gown of satin in the latest French shade of electric green with imported iridescent net and diamonds, and as the newspaper reported, it was all "most elaborate and exceedingly becoming." Asparagus fern entwined the chancel rail. Low pillars of white chrysanthemums and ferns tied with tulle outlined the chancel entrance, and from the choir loft rose "Ave Maria," devotional hymn to the Virgin, sung by a friend of the bride. Mildred wore a gift from her groom, a necklace of pearls and diamonds. The album was filled as well with lacy place-markers, paper figures of brides, grooms, attendants, names penned in elegant script, a vision to behold in an era when lacy place-markers mattered.

I always thought the Old Man was pleased beyond imagining at the wedding of his son Will to the society belle Mildred Foster. Somehow, it sealed the ascent to a grand life, "a player piano life," my father always said, a life where your travels to Palm Springs and your wife's teas would be written up in the newspaper society pages. My father always called that wedding "a spectacle of nineteenth-century upper-middle-class respectability at its

Developing Image 1

Thoughts West

*They were both disappointed in their marriage, I am sure.
Will grew inward, perhaps remembering the promise of
Stanford. It was about 1932, the year I graduated from
high school that my mother's fantasies seemed to take over.
She stopped making me lunch. Stopped playing bridge.
Stopped giving teas. Never knew what I ate (sometimes
the more affluent 17-year-olds would buy me lunch).
I wandered a lot, on Saturdays to San Francisco, taking the
nickel ferry from the foot of Broadway, coming back with a
raging sunburn. She never knew where I was. There was a
certain youthful freedom in all this, of course, but I worried
about her flight from reality. I am sure she wondered where
all the stardust had gone, the magic of the beaded wedding.*

"How was your day, Billy?"

"Oh, fine."

But she never asked.

most grotesque." To me, the wedding album is evidence of lives once lived. Like the front-page death notice. Like the absence of angels. Pieces of some still imagined whole. The beaded wedding gown, which Mildred kept locked up in the chest with the album, now lies in my brother's house in rural Northern California, in the same chest, another sliver of heritage, a talisman, its magic stuck in time.

⟡

At the simple ceremony we held at the Old Man's gravesite, I read a short passage from Emerson, the one ending with "one blood rolls uninterruptedly in endless circulation through all men, as the water of the globe is all one sea, and, truly seen, its tide is one."

My father, who did everything quietly, was quietly amused. He was not at all fond of Old Man Hugh. He was there at the grave only because he loved me, wanted, perhaps, to humor me. My father lit a cigarette.

"Fascinating," he said. "I spend my whole life trying to rid myself of these people, and here you guys come, all these years later, trying to resurrect them."

He inhaled deeply, then blew out the smoke, a grand sigh of resignation.

"Imagine that."

Even today, I hear his words in low whispers ... *escaped* ... (*did he escape?*).

Escape ... escapade.

When he told the story, my grandfather spoke in the voice of untold things, a warmer, a more musical voice than when he asked my mother what he could do to help in the kitchen, when he told my father he'd have dark meat from the turkey and his Scotch on the rocks. Even the way he said the name *Howard*—a softness in the *r*, a gentleman's *r*—*Howahd*, and on the second syllable, his voice drifting up just a bit, not quite a question, but a grace note.

"It was the Jazz Age," my grandfather said.

I didn't yet know that the Jazz Age was when everything broke loose after the First World War, but even as a child of six, I knew what jazz meant. At night, when my brother and I were in bed, my mother and father played jazz records. Those nights as I drifted off to sleep, the phonograph crackled between songs and sometimes during songs. The crackling records is one of my favorite memories from those nights of safe sounds. I knew all the words to the songs—"Let's Do It (Let's Fall in Love)," Ella Fitzgerald's voice singing them.

"It was a time that sounded like dancing trumpets," my grandfather continued. "A bounce-in-the-step time." I could see it. I imagined the trumpets following Uncle Howard wherever he went.

"Your uncle Howard had a big shiny new car, with a top that folded down. All the girls liked to ride with him. He was proud of that car. And he always wore the finest linen suits."

"Like the elephant?"

"Just like the elephant."

"And then what?"

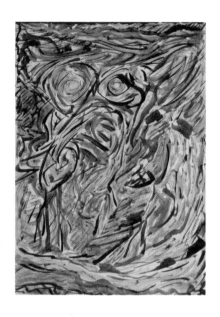

Digression
FROM MY FATHER'S NOTEBOOKS

The real and the unreal. You get into a philosophic
realm here. Real vs. unreal equals—memory? Memory
exaggerated, perhaps . . . Or was it a series of brief scenes,
magnified now . . . a girl asking me, "Did you just come
from the racetrack?" She was commenting on the clothes
I was wearing. I thought they were sharp . . . The scene
remains with me. Because of the humiliation, I think.
And the schoolmates who died in their teens. Three? Four?
Did they exist? But there they are, in my own tangled
memories, like the clothes. . . .

"Well—" My grandfather's voice dropped to a near whisper, his secret voice. "On this particular night, something happened—something terrible. And we know someone was with him in the car that night. But nobody ever knew."

"Why didn't they know?"

"Well, your uncle Howard ..." My grandfather removed his gold-rimmed glasses. His liquid blue eyes moved toward the ceiling. "Howard marched to a different drummer."

Uncle Howard even had a drummer! I imagined the drummer followed him wherever he went. It must have been a fine and wonderful sound. *Who was with him?* Over the years, this became my favorite part of the story. I kept asking, "Who?" even though I already knew the answer.

⟲

In the Jazz Age, on the day before the big thing happened to Uncle Howard, here is what I imagine people are saying:

talk of the town—

you read about those chicago boys?
leopold and loeb? rotten rich boys ... evil,
don't you think? people say the one's an
atheist, you can blame that on the parents
... all that sears and roebuck money ...
what kind of father would raise up a boy
like that, to bludgeon that child, just stuff
him in a ditch? ... it's in all the papers ...
they found the boy's shoes, for god's sake,
the little boy's shoes.

⟲

Such talk went on. It always does, in the barbershops, at the boathouses, the office buildings downtown, everywhere. They probably talked on the trolleys heading in and on the ferries drifting out, on the boulevards where silk-ruffled women lunched, and in parks where veterans told each other stories that were only vaguely true. They likely argued, sometimes wept, at the stories newspapers served up.

Nathan Leopold and Richard Loeb of Chicago, two young men, both from money, lots of money, who just for fun lured young Bobby Franks into their car, killed him with a chisel to the head, killed him and just for fun, they poured hydrochloric acid over his stripped-down body to see what it looked like. Just for fun, they stuffed him into a concrete drainage ditch then called the parents for a ransom.

Big news. Big gossip. A story this heinous, every barber, every cop and bartender, every businessman, even their wives, all had something to add. The evil in those boys. The alienists come to testify about their sanity. Clarence Darrow for the defense.

Then it stopped. The talk stopped. On the streets, in the homes, on the trolleys of Oakland, California, talk of Leopold and Loeb stopped on the morning of June 2, 1924, the moment the newspapers hit the sidewalk.

A new story about a rich kid, but this time he's local. Take the headlines, add people and imagination, and you have:

talk of the town—

*you read about the hogan boy? the car
crash? two dead, bodies crumpled up like
paper, they say. he is the son of mr. hogan
from the lumber company . . . built this city
. . . fine family . . . boy went to annapolis . . .
we know them, can you believe it? they say
he was drunk, smashed into the two men . . .
but the papers say someone else was in the
car, maybe two others, maybe the hogan
boy wasn't driving . . . this happens right
after those rich boys in chicago murdered
bobby franks, they'll get the noose for sure
. . . but the hogan boy, probably not the
noose . . . right?*

⊚

Noose, from the mid-fifteenth century, from the Old French, *no(u)s; nous,* meaning "knot." Knot, from *cnotta:* "intertwining or ropes, cords, etc." The stuff that binds, no matter what pries apart, smothers, or erases.

For a long time, America's instrument of capital punishment was the hangman's noose. It begins with a simple slipknot. The knot is ringed thirteen times. Noose makers found that thirteen coils, one atop the other, provided the perfect amount of pull to snap a person's neck.

Knot/noose. Ties that bind. Or kill.

Like families.

⊚

Of course, I never heard the din on the street, the talk on the trolley, how the mood of the crowd shifted, but I know it happened. My grandfather told me. He told me how everyone in town, meaning the city of Oakland, was talking about Howard, comparing what they knew, arguing—*did he really do it?*—did he really kill those two men with his shiny red Lincoln touring car, the car the ads said took every "hill on high and turned shorter than any other motorcar for its wheel base," the automobile my grandfather said all the girls wanted to ride in?

My grandfather Will was Howard's elder brother by eighteen years, practically raised Howard up himself, and had made it his job to be keeper of his baby brother's good name. He wanted me and my brother to know what really happened—or at least what did not happen—that night in 1924, so many years before but still fresh as new-sprung jonquils in my grandfather's mind. My grandmother Mildred in the background: "Now, don't you get those kids excited telling them your fanciful tales."

But he did.

My father lived on the edges of his past, a place of quieter slants, softer aches, sounds to sketch or write down. He remembered boarding an old vessel, patched up but sailable, steam pipes hissing, a spit and a clank, bound for Australia. In his later years, in the quiet of his backyard studio, he conjured the names of wood and steel ghosts he had known on the water: *Owl. Saldura. Hawaiian Farmer. Ever Gentle. Alligator Fortune.* They promised safety, deep passage to places with names that rang, Penang, Rangoon, Chankiang.

My father was always getting away on ships.

First, there were the real ships of his wanderings.

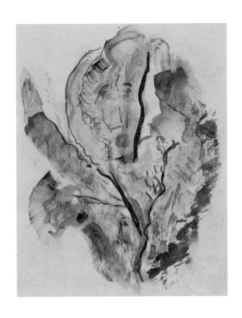

Moment Remembered

FROM MY FATHER'S NOTEBOOKS

Walking out of Our Lady of Lourdes Church in Oakland after listening to a particularly worthless sermon, age what? Almost 18? And thinking, the whole thing is a gigantic fraud. Which, of course, put me immediately on the defensive with my family. Or, as Hemingway put it in "A Moveable Feast" [Paraphrasing] ... With bad painters all you need to do is not look at them. But even when you have learned not to look at families nor to listen to them ... families have many ways of being dangerous.

Later, at least in my memory, he rode on ships of his dreaming, things recollected, remembered, notebook musings, thumbnail sketches, paintings to go with the words.

The Blue

FROM MY FATHER'S NOTEBOOKS

For instance, that July sunrise at the mouth of the Columbia River, Astoria, from the small steel hulled lumber vessel Munleon. The astonishing Blue of elsewhere, age 16.

At night, we'd sit in front of the driftwood fire, my father reminding us it's a sin to pay for firewood. On those nights, he would smoke, his cigarette ash growing longer and longer as he spoke, forgetting to flick the ash to the fire. The tumbler of white wine sat on the floor by his side, just within arm's reach. We would talk. One night I presented him with a treasure of my own, what I thought a treasure, at least—an album I had compiled of brittle yellowed news clippings about the 1924 manslaughter trial of his uncle Howard Hogan, my great-uncle, a man who died well before I was born, but about whom I had heard mythic stories since my earliest days.

Random Notes

The past, indeed. Gentler, somehow. In the philosophic
writings I have fooled around in, the question often arises:
Who am I? Strangely, I never asked myself that. I was
merely there, in some kind of story, like everyone else.
Perhaps a bit player in other people's stories. Somehow
I became my own story without really thinking about it.
I was me. But the Who? *There, with the images, the*
imaginings, the magnified memories? Never asked.
One needs a god here someplace.

My father opened the volume, scanned the headlines:

HOGAN ARRAIGNED FOR MEN'S DEATHS

Autoist Faces Charge of Manslaughter; Released on $20,000 Bond.

SURPRISE SPRUNG ON EVE OF HOGAN SLAYING TRIAL

FIGHT OPENS HOGAN AUTO DEATH CASE

"Fascinating," my father said. He quietly closed the album.

"Don't you want to read them?" I asked.

I had found the crumbling clippings in the bowels of the library at the *Oakland Tribune*, where I'd recently started working as a reporter. Uncle Howard's was a prominent, obscenely wealthy Oakland family back then. It was a handful of years before the Crash of '29, before their lives unraveled. Before it went up in a puff, all of it, the gentlemanly jobs, Carolinian chairs, silver serving platters, tea sets and fish forks, the brass door knockers, a player piano pumping out "The Merry Widow," the teas and garden parties in the society pages; a happiness, of sorts.

Sounds

FROM MY FATHER'S NOTEBOOKS

The Summer fogs. And foghorns when the wind is right, bringing to our hill the lingering lament from Angel Island, and beyond. Once in a while (a foggy while) a series of sounds—four, five, six—probably a nervous tanker headed down from the Contra Costa refineries? The wind must be just right. Usually night. Or early morning.

Howard's trial was as celebrated there in Oakland as the notorious capital murder case of Leopold and Loeb in Chicago, two sensational courtroom dramas going on at the same time. I pulled the original clippings about Howard from the *Oakland Tribune* library, replaced them with photocopies. I knew that no one would miss them. That was clear from how they were neatly placed in a brown paper envelope, each news clip expertly sliced from the full front page, neatly folded and placed, one behind the other. Nobody had opened that dusty file since the last story was clipped, folded, and inserted in 1926. Across the top of the envelope, in large typed letters: Howard Hogan, Auto Slayer.

"Oh, I'll read them," my father said. "In time."

But I knew he wouldn't. As fond as he had been of Uncle Howard, poring over those events—the verdict, the aftermath, the story he knew but never pursued—would take him back to the people he so wanted to be rid of. My father's yearnings for the distant harbors of his past had nothing to do with the ancestral clan he called "those poverty-stricken people choked in twisted nineteenth-century upper-middle-class values." He yearned instead for old street names, for smoky smells, movie tickets, the cost of a double ice cream, the yawn of an aging streetcar with room on the back for hitchhikers.

My father leaned forward in his black leather chair and flicked his cigarette ash into the fireplace, the soft dwindle of the fire. "Howard Hogan would make a fascinating novel, I think," he said, hoping to smooth the moment. He was aware, I am sure, that closing the album, my offering, hurt me.

Asides

FROM MY FATHER'S NOTEBOOKS

Groves of eucalyptus trees in the Piedmont Hills. Sounds of the inter-urban trains, the key route on a late afternoon; melancholy. The chill of a hearse, a funeral cortege moving up Piedmont Avenue, formerly, Cemetery Avenue.

Imagine. The whine of a peanut wagon. The iceman, and ice chips. Chewing tar from paving wagons. The view of the Magic City from the fronts of ferry boats. Tossing bread to the gulls, and their cries. I'm not sure of the thought here. Except that this is not a journal. And I would like to see an ice man.

"Of course, you'd have to be careful that you didn't over-Gatsby him. That would be the instinct, I think. But he was a dashing character, a kind of Gatsby, in a way, but you wouldn't want to overdo it."

"Did Howard ever tell you what really happened that night?" I asked.

"He never talked about it. Not a word. Mum. Ever the gentleman. He wanted the whole thing behind him. Who can blame him? He went on to become a brilliant surgeon, he had a life in Dallas there, with that Southern girl he married, that Sally, a nice girl. At least he never told me anything. Maybe your poor grandfather knew something, I really don't know. What I do know is that when Howard was dying of cancer, poor fellow—just forty-eight, imagine!—your aunt Betty went down to Texas to see him, to visit. Howard said, 'Tell your dear father—tell my brother Will—that the warrior came home on his shield.' Betty said she would. Then Betty asked him, 'Howard, what really happened that night, the night of the accident? Something happened, we know that. *What?* What was it?' Howard told her, 'We don't talk about that night. It's better, for us, for everyone, just to let that night lie.'"

⊚

The warrior came home on his shield. I wanted to know what it meant. I searched Shakespeare. Nothing. Then years later, I found in an anthology an essay about Spartan mothers, by Plutarch. The mothers, he wrote, would tell their sons before they went off to war: "Come home either with your shield, or on it."

⊚

Maritime Thoughts

FROM MY FATHER'S NOTEBOOKS

Phyllis suggested a series of reminiscences on San Francisco when it was still a world port. But where would one start? Maritime notes? (There is a question mark, for it all relies on memory.) You could start from seeing, from the cupola of your grandmother's house, scow schooners coming up from Alviso with deck loads of hay and produce, or oyster shells, heading toward the Petaluma River. All this, of course, is raw material, which you must analyze and form into some sort of narrative. I wonder, too, who might be interested ... The river boats still ran in the '20s. And the Steamer Gold to Petaluma. And the Owl to Bolinas ... Maybe you could start with that.

FROM MY FATHER'S NOTEBOOKS

Memory is not good enough to sketch it. Matisse could do
it. There was a lot of purple, especially in the afternoon,
and always shadows. And white. Yes, Matisse could have.
The doorways with beads. Eyes above veils. Goats. Stone
stairways. Chanting prayer. Signs at the entrance to
The Quarter: Off limits!" The story was that a soldier in
there, a knife in his back, had everything on him but his
leather boots. Casbah Algiers, 1942.

My father went back to the fire fed by his driftwood, to his habit of summoning the groan of distant ships. "I've been reading in a wonderful book," he said, "about how the steam schooners were holdovers from the nineteenth century. The ferryboats, too. The Thoroughfare, on which I crossed a few times, was built in the 1870s, and scrapped in the 1930s, I think. I remember seeing some of the West Coast lumber ships in the bay from the ferryboats or from the docks on the Oakland estuary. I remember their names: *Capistrano, Daisy Gray, Helen P. Drew. Quinault,* and of course, the old *Noyo.* Great names."

The time, the place, and the girl. My father loved that phrase. He heard it from an old press agent who'd worked on a Broadway show of the same name. "The time, the place, and the girl," he would say. "A marvelous thing."

It meant that serendipitous moment when God was smiling down, the stars hung from magical corners on high, and you just so happened to come along. He often told us that was how it was, the time, the place, and the girl, during the war, when he was a corporal in the 1st Armored Division, in Tunisia, as it turns out. A letter arrived, with orders, telling him to report to Rome where he would join the staff of the *Stars and Stripes.* He'd applied to the newspaper months before, heard nothing, and forgot about it.

"Then came the famous orders," he would say, "and somehow, my life changed." He rested his M-1 against a tree, threw his bag over his shoulder, flagged down a GI truck, climbed on, hitchhiking all the way to Rome. Rome, Sicily, Palermo, Mondello, even North Africa—they became the places of his dreams, like the ships; villages, scenes, beaches he traveled back to in reverie, for solace, to remember.

Palermo, an ancient coastal town in Sicily, was where my father found his angel, unearthed from the rubble of a bombed-out church. The angel stands just under a foot high, crimson shawl rippling around his back and fluttering toward his face. He doesn't have wings. "Real angels never did," my father said. But he looks in midflight, God's crimson-robed messenger heading off to spread some urgent news. My father rescued the angel, carefully placed it in his bag, hoping he wasn't technically stealing from the Vatican, and brought it back to California, wrapped in newspaper. It remained there, in a bottom desk drawer, until my parents found enough money to have it mounted and encased in a plastic box. The angel from Palermo, he often said, was a case of the time, the place, and the girl. He hung it in the entryway to the house. He called it the House Angel, and said it watched over us always.

As I was leaving one evening, I looked up at the angel on the wall.

"Daddy," I said, "your angel is dusty."

My father said, "So who isn't?"

NAMING

"Can you believe," my father once told me, "that Old Man Hugh named one of his lumber schooners the *Hugh Hogan?* Imagine!—imagine naming a ship after yourself! What gall. What *chutzpah*. What lack of imagination!"

The *Hugh Hogan* was a three-masted schooner, 392 tons, with capacity to carry thousands of pounds of timber, one of several of the shoal-draft schooners in the Old Man's fleet. She wrecked off the Oregon coast in 1922. No one hurt, nothing salvaged.

Future driftwood.

Stories of Great Prosperity

EXCERPT FROM AN *OAKLAND TRIBUNE*
FEATURE STORY, JANUARY 11, 1911

*As sometimes on a winter's day an acorn
shaken from the oak and buffeted by
the wind finds lodgment in a cleft, so
sometimes . . . an individual arrives . . .
bringing with him the acorn of potentiality,
which, warmed by the sunshine of business
ability, sustained by the air of application
and sprayed with the moisture of energy,
makes for the growth of business. . . .*

*Hugh Hogan came to Oakland, where he
formed the Humboldt Lumber Company,
the acorn from which sprung the Hogan
Lumber Company, an Oak which storms
of rivalry and competition have not been
able to overthrow.*

It began, I suppose, with the Book of Genesis, where God
has a soft spot for patriarchs. In the industrial age, the men
of means collect the blessings—men with names like Crocker,
Rockefeller, Astor, J. P. Morgan, Vanderbilt, Carnegie, and even
though he never made it into the history books, Old Man Hugh.
God-given prosperity would rain down on those who grabbed

hold of the biblical dictum that Man "have dominion over all things that creepeth" on this earth, meaning the fish of the sea, the fowl of the air, the cattle, or in the Old Man's case, that which reached up to scrape the skies, the trees.

The book *Greater Oakland, 1911,* a civic inventory of the dizzying promise of it all, presented the city as the proud manufacturing muscle of the San Francisco Bay Area. Not only the Standard Oil refinery and the Pullman Car Company, but pipe works and iron works and shipbuilding plants, as well as manufactories of sashes, doors, flax seed oil, oil cake, and "a thousand and one enterprises in which raw material is modified and transformed for the use and service of men."

The ethos of thing-ness, the essence of Old Man Hugh.

The son of Irish immigrants, the Old Man may never have read a book in his life, but he grew good and rich through his natural gift for calculating dollars per thousand board feet of every pine, redwood, and oak long before tree ever met crosssaw. I always imagined that he saw trees as things, as *its*, in the same way, according to my father, that he saw his children. An *it* had a purpose, obedience, say, not this particular son with his particular gifts and flaws, God help him if he had flaws. An *it* rather than a pine, sacred to Native peoples of America as well as the Taoists of China, a fact I feel sure he never knew. An *it* rather than a redwood, which in Native California cultures, symbolized balance, the weaving of heaven and earth into one happily rooted family of trees.

He simply calculated the utility of each, how that would translate to wealth. He was pleased, I am sure, the day a news reporter came to interview him about the state of lumber in the city, pleased at having a chance to think lofty thoughts, to say them for the people of the city, maybe even for posterity.

In the *Oakland Tribune* feature story, the Old Man spoke:

> *The first mention we have anywhere*
> *of the use of wood products is in the*
> *Bible account of the expulsion from*
> *Eden, where Eve is said to have made*
> *for herself a covering of leaves. And*
> *since then, wood and its products have*
> *been one of the greatest boons to mankind.*
>
> *His first weapon was the gnarled branch*
> *of a tree, which he used as a club. His*
> *first boat, a log. When one of our cave-*
> *men forefathers, in leaning over a log*
> *to catch fish, separated it from the*
> *landing, and found it would bear his*
> *weight, by paddling with his hands . . .*
> *he discovered propulsion on the water . . .*

When I first read the Old Man's interview, I thought of the naming of things. In particular, of trees, Carolina ash, spruce, hickory, coast live oak, maple, each with its own mythology, its own spirit, its own purpose on the earth, its own role in nature's narrative. I think of our mystical banyan trees in Florida, their name reflecting not a type of tree (they are various species of fig), but rather the way it grows. A banyan starts as a seed that a wind or a passing bird drops into a crevice in a standing tree, maybe a cabbage palm. There in that cradling cranny, the seed sprouts, sending down aerial roots, tendrils springing out, reaching down, aching to connect with the earth. As they grow earthward, each root thickens, each tendril builds on the others around it. And so, the forming tree, the banyan, grows some legs to stand on. The tendrils crisscross, mingle, intertwine, descend from the mother branch, and before you know it, dozens, sometimes hundreds of roots, all from the one seed, are now indistinguishable from their mother. They have become their own forest: *One.*

We had just moved to Florida. My then-twelve-year-old, William, named after my father, encountered the tangled sprawl of a banyan at the park.

"Look at that!" William said. "It's—it's a *God Tree!*"

In the beginning, Genesis says, God gave Adam and Eve "every tree that is pleasant to the sight, and good for food." Trees, but no names, but for the Tree of Knowledge and the Tree of Life. No fig, no peach nor plum, no cedar, sugar pine, or redwood, no banyan for a child to call "a God Tree."

After the Fall of Man, humanity could name trees, give them a purpose, turn trees into cities, into civilizations. Trees to make art. To build temples. To learn to forgive and, maybe, to discover grace.

Read Genesis literally, and the Garden of Eden was a swell place.

"Pure and sweet," as the poet Andrew Marvell put it:

> *Here at the fountain's sliding foot,*
> *Or at some fruit tree's mossy root,*
> *Casting the body's vest aside,*
> *My soul into the boughs does glide;*
> *There like a bird it sits and sings,*
> *Then whets, and combs its silver wings;*
> *And, till prepar'd for longer flight,*
> *Waves in its plumes the various light.*
>
> *Such was that happy garden-state . . .*

Eden. A place nobody would ever want to leave. Why should they? Relax all day, pick whatever unspecified fruit happened to beckon, stay happily naked, and every so often, check in with God, the deity in residence. Things would be fine so long as you followed the rules; sort of a giant bliss factory, with God as semibenevolent foreman, making sure no one was skimming from the till. Break the rules: eternal downfall.

Read it as a parable, and the lessons of Genesis change. Humankind was given knowledge, consciousness, and all the pain that came with it. But along with that came writing and imagination and the ability to put our lives into poetry, on paper.

In a poem my father and I talked about often, Robert Frost describes Adam hearing a difference in the way the birds sounded after Eve joined him there. Adam had been listening to Eve's voice, the rise and fall of her laughter, and in a transformational instant, he discovered that birdsong possessed a new sort of beauty, "an oversound." Frost ends: "Never again would birds' song be the same. / And to do that to birds was why she came."

"Wonderful line," my father would say each time. "Marvelous."

In Frost's version of the story, Eve doesn't bring about the Fall of Man by eating from the Tree of Knowledge. Instead, she brings meaning, to apples, birds, and the trees they live in. She brings music, memory, the names of things, the beginning of races, of human consciousness.

My father and I would talk about Eve walking though the gardens of the world, bestowing on each tree a name, something it didn't have before. So the cedar became the cedar, meant for building the Ark of the Covenant, and the oak became the oak, meant for something else uniquely *oak*, a blessing. Because when you name something, a piece of prairie land, a boat, a child, you imbue it with value, purpose, with hope. In that Eden, knowledge of good and evil brings not exile but a choice. Those bent on greed and destruction can come along to count their gold. But because of Eve, who added the oversound, we can build and dream in spite of them.

Naturalists say that when a banyan tree is hat-racked (meaning, pruned, shaped, cut back ornamentally to conform to someone's idea of what a tree should look like), it weakens. The hat-racked trees can tumble over in hurricanes because their true nature has been compromised, subjugated to the will of the city's tree people or an overzealous gardener. Let the tree be what it is meant to be, they say, not how you want it to be. Trim it back to how you want it to look, how you want it to behave, and surely it will fall.

I was baptized at Our Lady of Mount Carmel Catholic Church in downtown Mill Valley, California, and given a very Catholic name, Mary Ann, the name of the Blessed Virgin and her mother. I wore the same hand-stitched cotton-lace baptismal gown my mother had worn as a baby, the same gown my brother wore, which my brother's daughter wore, and which my own two sons wore when they were christened, not in the Church like my brother and me, but in front of my parents' brick fireplace in an offbeat ceremony led by a Protestant pastor with a drop of pagan in him.

My being baptized and named in the Church had nothing to do with my parents believing in Catholicism. It had everything to do with my father wanting to please his mother. Grandmother Mildred of the beaded wedding gown would not have spent one

Theology West

Don't eat a hot dog on Friday, they told us (with straight faces). A sin. Don't think impure thoughts. A sin. What, wondered the ten-year-old boy, is an impure thought? Why did God, who created Heaven and Earth, object to hot dogs? On Fridays? If a child wasn't baptized, he went to "Limbo" after his death. "Limbo?" A mystery, said the priests. There were so many mysteries. Well, I was baptized. And if I conquered "Sloth," for example, I was Okay, no Limbo there. But what about all those Chinese people? The Hottentots and things? Never a chance of Heaven. Poor devils.

restful day if her only grandchildren hadn't been granted official entry into the Kingdom of Heaven. Even if they lived full lives, dying as old folks, the unbaptized would be trotted off to Limbo, the border of Hell, for an eternity, give or take a few. There they would hang with the dead babies whisked there for the same eternity.

By the time my own sons were christened in front of the fireplace, Grandmother Mildred, along with her husband, my grandfather Will, had slipped into the ancestral stew that marinated my father's psyche.

Maybe ten or fifteen years after that, the place named Limbo was eliminated by papal decree. The pope said it had always been theological hypothesis only, so what was the difference? He signed on the dotted line. Limbo was gone, erased, as if it had never existed. My father would have loved the story. Eternity, edited with the stroke of the holy pen.

◕

...What is thy name? And he said, Jacob.

*And he said, Thy name shall be called no
more Jacob, but Israel: for as a prince hast
thou power with God and with men ...*

And he blessed him there.

*And Jacob called the name of the place
Peniel: I have seen God face to face,
And my life is preserved.*

—Gen. 32:27–30

Our son James was born in 1993, in Oakland, California, the city where my father was born, where Old Man Hugh named a lumber schooner after himself, and where the early Hogan family brought in tons of timber to build up a city in place of the oak groves. We named him James after two of my father's favorite writers, James Joyce and James Baldwin. We named him James because James is a strong name, the name of poets and writers and kings; James, the English version of the Hebrew Jacob, the supplanter and heel-grabber, grandson of Abraham. Jacob, whose name was changed to Israel, stood in a place he called Peniel, meaning "Face of God."

Like his brother before him, James was born by Caesarean section. He came perhaps a week too soon. His breathing wasn't right, wasn't rhythmic. They took him from me and put him in the ICU a few doors down from my room. I lay in a hospital bed, and they took my baby James and placed him in a glass box, monitors on his chest and legs. I went down to see him every hour, but I couldn't hold him.

"He'll be fine," the doctor said. "We just want to watch him for a few days. He may be fine tomorrow." I went back to my hospital room. A nurse came in with lunch.

"Now what do you got to be crying about, honey?" she said. "You have a beautiful boy."

"He's in the ICU. I'm worried. I want my baby back."

"Oh, honey girl, these doctors, they know what they're doing, he'll be fine, he's in ICU, they watch him every minute, he's never alone. They won't let nothin' happen to your baby, you'll see."

I started to eat my Jell-O.

"*Nooo*," the nurse went on, "ICU is where he should be, they know what to do. You don't have a thing to worry about. Only time you have to start worrying is if they take him to Children's.

Yeah, if they take the baby to Children's, that's when you worry, but here in ICU, he'll be just fine, honey, just fine."

As she left, she said, maybe to herself, "Yeah, when they take 'em to Children's, that's when you worry, but so long as he's here and he ain't goin' to Children's, you got nothing to worry, nothing at all."

A doctor came in.

"We're taking the baby to Children's Hospital. We have a medical transport team coming right now to transfer the baby. I need you to sign these release forms for the transfer."

We're taking the baby to Children's. Did I scream? Or was it just a cry? I know it was bigger than a cry, as in cry tears. It was audible—a wail? Was someone holding me? Was I shaking? Seven men, big men, seven big men in heavy gear. Were they paramedics? Were they wearing boots? They were there in my hospital room, I counted them, seven, one pushing the glass box on a cart with my baby inside as I signed forms, signed surrounded by seven big men wearing gear and a baby under glass and someone holding me. They left, pushing the glass box on a cart, going to the ambulance, the waiting ambulance that will speed, sirens blasting, four miles down the road to Children's Hospital and Research Center, the place where they take the babies and, when they do, then you can start to worry.

That nurse promised me, she told me God wouldn't bring forth such a child, whose name was changed to Israel, without letting him live to his full glory. I first held him in my arms five days after he was born. Looked down into his eyes, deep and somehow knowing. I thought, this child of mine is an old soul, one that has traveled and learned as he went.

Struggles

FROM MY FATHER'S NOTEBOOKS

Please be well, little James, and come home soon, so I can hold you in my aging arms. Think of it—my grandchild of the twenty-first century. James! What a marvelous name. Will you be a writer one day? Unlike your poor old PopPop, who had dreams? What wonders will you see in the century to come? Please, let there be wonders. Less chaos, more light. Like the old prayer says. "May perpetual light shine upon you." I just hope I live long enough so you can know your old PopPop. I hope all your ships are good ships with proper names.

Six years later, James and I were walking down the nature trail a few blocks from our brick- and vinyl-sided Virginia house, which sat on a third of an acre with thirty trees that changed color and shed their leaves in the fall in a way I had never seen in California. Sun rays streaked through the thicket of forest. There was a fall wind—a Virginia fall, a Virginia wind—and then, one by one, up toward the trees in airy parade, downy dandelion puffs floated skyward.

"James—look!" I said. "Look at the dandelion puffs—they're like fairies. *Fairies!* in our forest."

James watched the parade in the streaks of sun. The look on his face was familiar, the same as when I first held him in my arms, the same eyes, as if he were looking to a realm beyond, someplace elsewhere.

"You wanna know a secret?" he said.

"Yeah. Tell me. What's your secret?"

"When I was a lot younger, like maybe four, I used to think those fairy puffs were souls."

My father would have loved that story. Would have told it to everyone he knew, would have painted the fairy puffs in his notebooks. He would have smiled his half smile, and said, "Now, *that's* what I call the word of God."

SWIRL

Palm Beach County, Florida, 2005, morning of the storm

The TV newscasts have stopped.

Electricity went out sometime last night.

I have lost count of the hours. Shadowed light filters in from the morning, but the sky is mostly black. How to imagine, to see, to feel the coming of a 125-mile-an-hour wind? You are a boat, pulled down and around into the vortex Charybdis, the sucking, the spinning, can't catch your breath, can't hold on, whirling down, thoughts plummeting, otherworldly, helpless. Right now, a huge thing streaks by overhead, bigger than a giant lost bird—the birdcage enclosure from our next-door neighbor's swimming pool, flying past, just missing us. But the whistle sounds, the whistling sound, like fireworks I remember as a five-year-old, screaming, incessant, reeling, *Why won't it stop?* The trees have turned to furies, hair streaking behind their snapping heads, bending, almost horizontal, bowing down before Huracán. On our hand-crank radio we hear a woman in the north part of the county was killed when a projectile (mango? brick?) flew through a window. We hear that the shattering glass, the sheets of glass flying into her house, almost sliced her body in half.

"Oh shit," my husband says. "We shoulda put up all the shutters."

It is hot in the house, humid. It is black outside. There is pounding. Huge clank, pounding. The barbecue, the five-hundred-pound propane grill my children gave me last year on Mother's Day so we could grill chicken outside on the patio in front of the pool. An offering from my husband, who knew I didn't want to live here in a pastel terra-cotta suburban home behind locked gates. We have brought in the oranges, the coconuts, my father's driftwood, but we have not brought in the barbecue, and right now it is clanking, lopsided, sides banging, heaving against a few old shutters slapped into place over our glass French doors; the doors are old, too, we should have replaced them, the doors leading to the patio, and with each banging of the barbecue in the demon wind—the shutters give, the doors bulge and nearly buckle.

We will hear that the woman who was almost sliced in half by flying glass is just one of many people in the county who were alive one day and dead the next. We have heard about the deadliest hurricane in recorded history, more than two centuries ago, roughly a thousand miles south of our Florida home. Death toll: twenty-two thousand. But right now, we are not dead, not yet, and wonder if we should move to the closet stocked with blankets and pillows, water and cat food. But would it matter? (We have also read that hurricanes can release as much energy as ten thousand nuclear bombs.) The storm, the battery-powered radio says, is moving across the county. Soon, the entire expanse of Palm Beach County, Florida, will lie, stonily quiet, under eye of the hurricane, until the real furies come.

The Hubble Space Telescope, my scientist friend observes, captures extraordinarily detailed images of spiral galaxies—celestial swirls and whirlpools, heavenly funnels that spin through the far reaches of the universe. I think about those galaxies as I study my father's notebooks, imagining his hand moving in a circular motion over the pages where he drew frenzies of spirals, loops, and curves spilling out from jars, into holes, into the air. One drawing about the spiral inside his head he titled, "This Is How Thoughts Fly."

He collected shells, was charmed by the nautilus, "the most elegant spiral in nature," one suggesting continuous creation, eternity. The jellylike creature inside the shell inches itself into each new chamber of growth, much as humans do when they allow themselves to. Maybe that's what my father was thinking when he drew his swirls. His own continuous creations, thoughts unmoored as his pen skipped across the pages, burrowing into his past, trolling the deep running currents of his psyche. Or was it an intellectual joke (so like him)? Had he seen in the *Columbia Encyclopedia* that great minds of science and literature studied vortical shapes in nature? That poets from Dante to Blake to

Pound to Yeats saw the vortex as a symbol of emergence, wholeness, transcendence, as well as destruction? Even Yahweh, one of his favorite gods, spoke through a big swirl: "Then the Lord answered Job out of the whirlwind, and said, Who is this that darkeneth counsel by words without knowledge?" The nautilus he treasured, now resting on the entry-hall table in my Florida home, ran in august company. My father would have liked that. Would have loved that his sea treasure had something in common with Yahweh.

I have lived through my own swirling thoughts and often wonder if my father's were anything like mine. I remember the first one, the musty smell of the day. I was in the city room of the *Oakland Tribune*. Working on a story about the county jail. No idea what I was doing. Suffocating doubt. *When did it start?* Smiling, always smiling. Good at pretending. Then it came, quicksand in the veins.

Have to lie down somewhere couch is somewhere how to escape when thoughts start to fly fireworks bursting scraping inside the head loud colors and blacks and whites chest heavy, arms shaky lungs in vise, air gone face numb whole body sucked down to nothing

Someone called 911.

The couch was in the ladies' room.

I always felt my newspaper career was a fluke. No formal training. Yet I grew up in a house drenched in books and writing and nightly talk of interviews, authors, deadlines, the next day's paper. Like ether enveloping you from birth. You breathe

This is How Thoughts Fly...

Brief Memories

FROM MY FATHER'S NOTEBOOKS

*Things are moving fast. Thoughts well up, flying, spiraling,
things I haven't thought about in years. Just notes, of
course, nothing more. Autobiography must be a pain in
the neck. How does one really know how he felt, thought,
acted, performed, 50 years ago—30, 10 years? If this
(as Hemingway wrote) could have been enough of a book ...
But it is not a book. Not autobiography. After I left the
newspaper, people asked, "Don't you miss the by-lines?"
No, I left that to my daughter Mary Ann. She is not as lazy
as her father. Not the dreamer, either—as his father was.
What a legacy. (Just dream a little, Mary Ann.)*

it, it seeps in. First came a handful of features for a local paper, then a few freelance magazine assignments. And then, oddest luck, strange magic, a daily newspaper job. "Imagine that!" I remember my father saying. "My child going out there to God knows where to interview inmates at the jail!"

Over the years I brought him stories I wrote, offerings, knowing they would delight him, for a moment, at least, before he deflated again. *"Brilliant!"* he would say, before he even read a word. (Did he actually read them, or just look at the byline?) *"Brilliant!"* I didn't think the stories were at all brilliant, just adequate, workmanlike. But in his mind, they meant I was on my way to succeeding him, that I would finish his unfinished business, somehow complete him.

A few weeks after my Oakland city-room calamity, I lay on a blanket in my mother's poppy patch in the backyard of my parents' 1950s post-and-beam house, the house I grew up in. I was in the garden because I needed air. Because of the flying thoughts and heavy chest and quicksand in the veins and people who ask me things, it had grown into a nature force, a hurricane in my head, a storm that started with a simple swirl, gathering speed, then more, then when I went out in the world, people asking me what I was doing, and in a second, the landscape starting to fly, objects and thoughts streaking by. All of a sudden I could not leave my parents' house.

I took the tiny dark-green pills someone prescribed. In a day or so, I no longer had flying thoughts, or any thoughts at all. Just numbness, fuzzy, couldn't remember, couldn't pick up a glass, or a pen, but then, why would I need to? No need, because my mother was there, holding my head up. She would hold the glass, or the pen, she held a milkshake, told me to sip, but I couldn't remember how to swallow.

"How do people talk?" I asked her.

My father came home from work. Found us out back in the garden. Asked my mother how his little girl was doing. My father, the newspaperman, never liked bad news. It assaulted his fragile Irish senses. Made his chest sink. Made him smoke with more fury.

Over the years he told us, "One of these days, I'm going to have a radio station that only tells the good news. I'll only have headlines like, 'Healthy Baby Born.' 'College Graduate Finds Good Job.' 'Americans Happy with How Things Are.' 'Beach Cleaned Up Good.'"

"But, Daddy, what if someone we know, what if one of us, has a horrible job or marriage or drops dead or goes broke or something?"

"Then you can't be on my radio station."

My mother learned early on not to tell him bad things, knowing it would shake his already rickety frame. She would never tell him that his child couldn't lift her head up or leave the garden or swallow or pick up a pen, so she told him, "Much better, I think" when he asked how his daughter was, so then he could say "Thank God" and go inside. Inside, he would pour himself a bourbon on ice, light a Kent, maybe consult with his Angel. Then he would retreat to his artist studio out back, where he would read, watch the rhythms of his garden, sleep off the imagined enemy volleys of the day.

◎

Weeds

FROM MY FATHER'S NOTEBOOKS

Digging weeds out of the back patch of garden, a daily deadline. But I find myself retreating, discouraged. Retreating from the physical violence against the weeds, their grotesque matted root growth, which I no longer have strength to control. Spring and then the rains and then the weeds. They are heartier than ever this season. Mats and tangles of them. And tough. They astonish me. Dozens of varieties. I recognize them by now. And I think they recognize me—smiling, maybe laughing. Laughing weeds. When the silly human race is a forgotten species, Weeds will remain. But yet ... yet, what a great affirmation of life, bursting up like that between the cracks in the planter boxes. (They have already outlasted me, whether they know it or not.)

I think back to that time, the darkest time of my swirling thoughts, and wonder where they came from. Whether my father's fragile moorings, his barricading himself against the world, our complicity in shielding him, created it, fed it, had anything to do with it. Whether his crippling self-doubt somehow spun down to me.

Whether his had spun down from his own father, my grandfather Will.

Maybe the poet Blake had the answer when he said, "The nature of Infinity is this: That every thing has its / Own Vortex." Maybe he meant the vortex of one's own life is interlinked with that of one's family, with that family's past, their intertwined histories shedding debris—fears and unfinished business, secrets and wounds—as the generations cycle down. Could be.

My scientist friend tells me that fear defines the human lot. That people either channel it, transform it into something productive (a lumber empire, say), or allow it to churn in the veins, turning everyday slights into phantom predators a hundred feet tall. Whether we channel or churn depends on everything. Genetics, environment, personality, the thousand forces that shape us, our ability to manage the difference between how things seem and the way we sense they really are.

Images from my early childhood are mostly pleasant, happy even. The horse farm where my father took us for riding lessons. I remember a tall red horse named Sam. Trips to the driftwood beach where he taught us to search and to run from the waves. The sound of my mother's chopping in a wooden bowl, warm, safe smells from her kitchen, homemade yellow cake with chocolate frosting on the back patio on foggy Fourths of July, always fog on the Fourth. But I also remember unsettling shifts in the small landscapes of childhood life, moments where meaning and marrow didn't mesh. The sound of my mother's voice when she greeted my grandfather Will on holidays: "Hello, Will, dear, how nice to see you … Can I get you anything, dear?" It was not my mother's voice. Not the home-made-yellow-cake voice I knew. The voice was hollow, chilled, a pretend voice. *Where did my mother's voice go? Why doesn't she like Papa?*

Later I would describe the feeling as walking down a stone path, the stones turning to lily pads, and you'd sink to the murk, a place of unknowing. Later still I would think: If we were such a happy family, as I thought us to be, then why did I have to try so hard, so often to make my father happy?

Daddy, why were you always getting away on ships?

I remember other lily-pad moments. As children, my brother and I would visit our grandparents and Aunt Betty, my father's unmarried sister, in their one-bedroom apartment just across the Golden Gate Bridge in San Francisco. The apartment was filled with remnants of the onetime wealth of their family, a world that vanished, scattered by the wind, as my father always said, "just like the treasure of the Sierra Madre." Nothing left but stale disappointment.

A few relics to remind them there was once a fine time:

A collection of cut-glass perfume bottles.

A photograph of my father as a young man in a carved antique silver frame.

Hummel figurines of children and angels.

Chairs with elaborately carved wooden feet, and cushions with pink and orange flowers in achingly delicate needlepoint.

My grandfather Will didn't really live in the apartment with my grandmother and Betty. He lived down the hall in a tiny studio, a bed that rolled out from the wall at night, folded back up in the day. Just came to the apartment when we were visiting. Why? Nobody ever said. Nobody ever said anything about Grandfather Will and Grandmother Mildred not speaking directly to each other, though Mildred treasured that black leather album of the orange-blossomed wedding.

Sometimes my grandfather would take me and my brother out to dinner in downtown San Francisco at his favorite café. It was all glass in front, and inside, tall linoleum-topped tables and giant steel tubs, bigger than sinks, overflowing with mashed potatoes, gravy, sliced turkey, and roast beef; meatballs, corn bread, and macaroni and cheese. The place was warm, full of pleasant older men, white shirts and hats, gentlemen, like our papa, shaking hands with him, with us, before we stuffed ourselves on mashed potatoes and gravy and corn bread.

"Don't be little piggies, now," my grandfather would say.

I loved going to the glass-front downtown café, a grand treat, an adventure, with Papa in his three-piece brown tweed suit, pocket watch in the vest, attached to a real gold chain. It was better than a palace, I always thought, grander, certainly, than anything we ever did at home.

I later came to know that our mashed-potato café was where old men ate when there was no nowhere else to go.

Will R. Hogan, My Father

FROM MY FATHER'S NOTEBOOKS

*Will R. Hogan. The lovable victim. The original Pied
Piper. All the fiddle players in all the Gaelic pubs of all
time. All these threads ... But that. Guilt? I thought that
had evaporated when he visited me in New York in 1945.
Breakfast at the Waldorf, courtesy of his son Billy, the
kid with the ribbons on his tunic. Symbols. But my father
seemed happier than he had been in years.*

*The guilt must come later after thinking about it—him.
I analyze this guilt ... What am I guilty of? It never quite
went away. I didn't—and don't—know what the guilt is.
I must think about it before articulating anything that
might bring Will R. Hogan into focus. But somehow,
I am* my father.

Long before that:

Old Man Hugh's wife, the patient Anna, would read him everything he needed to know. News of the day, the business columns, stocks and lumber prices, shipping news, society pages, the travels and bridge games and teas of his fellow members of the Knights of Columbus and their silken wives; politics of the state and the world, how it all trickled down to the way great men lived their lives.

My father remembers the Old Man saying, "There's such a thing as too much education, you know."

From what I can piece together, the Old Man was nothing if not secure, in his wealth, in his faith, in his control over family, in his business, in his grasp of the utilitarian value of a thing, whether a dollar, a tree, or a son. I imagine he thought his older son, my grandfather Will, weak, not built for the stern stuff of business, retreating, as he did, into Tolstoy, Dostoevsky, the chroniclers of Russian and European history, the world of ideas, a world Will glimpsed at Stanford, one that had no place in the second-story office of Old Man Hugh's lumberyard. It was there that my grandfather submitted to his father, working in a series of jobs: yard manager, ledger keeper, maintenance operative, inventory checker, mill operations captain, inventory advisor, anything the Old Man could justify with a title and a desk and a paycheck. When my grandfather went to the lumberyard, I imagine, he went not so much to work as to pass the time, the gentleman scion in a fine tweed suit and with gold pocket watch. He went to avoid the Old Man's scorn, his belittling, to make sure he didn't lose out on the money as he waited for the day when the dull tasks would end. Because, if you waited long enough, things might change, they just might.

◎

Will R. Hogan II

FROM MY FATHER'S NOTEBOOKS

Will was a dreamer, a kind of semi-intellectual who somehow got himself (I don't know how) into Stanford for a year or two. He loved Stanford. Should have gone on to become a professor of history, or literature, damn it. Instead, became a well-dressed bum. No support, for one thing, from that anti-intellectual father of his, Old Man Hugh. No formal education there, and not a jot of imagination. The Old Man insisted that Will go into the lumber business, which he hated. Will didn't have a shred of business sense. He knocked around in a variety of menial lumber-company jobs, hating every minute of it, and, I suppose, waiting for the Old Man to drop dead so maybe he could take the money, start over, live the life of a gentleman reader of Tolstoy. What a legacy, indeed.

The Old Man, I am sure, knew every disease, every entomological assault, that could befall a tree, bring blemishes to render it useless for lumber. He would have known the black locust as a highly prized hardwood, rot resistant, excellent for making railway ties. Not many, though, could be found. That's because the locust borer, a bark-gnawing grub, would twist its way into the stem of the young tree, mutilating it, sapping its essence, sucking out the life it could have had, making the tree gnarled, stunted, useless for building railroad ties or anything else of value.

A tree without an Angel.

I never heard my grandfather mention Old Man Hugh's name.

LITERARY CARGO

My father sat in a jet five miles above Bingham Canyon, Utah, writing notes on copy paper clamped atop a clipboard. The year: 1963. Next to him sat that day's interview, James Baldwin, the American writer well on his way to becoming a legend.

"It's fabulous," Baldwin said. "A magnificent country."

"Yes, indeed," my father said.

That day in 1963, Baldwin peered out the window. "Wouldn't it be wonderful if the government could send hundreds of jets loaded with schoolchildren, kids who never get a chance, to see their own country? Nobody really sees his own country."

Later, after the acclaim that came with *The Fire Next Time*, Baldwin would say, to another interviewer:

> *I believe—what do I believe? I believe in*
> *... I believe in love ... I mean something*
> *active, something more like a fire, like the*
> *wind, something which can change you.*
> *I mean energy. I mean a passionate belief,*
> *a passionate knowledge of what a human*
> *being can do, and become.*

I wish my father could have felt that same fire, the same wind that changes a person, that might have changed him. But in that jet, at that moment, James Baldwin was talking through a journalist, my father, to a nation, talking about changing at least a sliver of a world for thousands of inner-city children, some of whom, at that same moment, many miles away in the American South, were getting hosed down by police in the so-called Battle of Birmingham. It was the pivotal event of the American civil rights movement, and the reason Baldwin had returned to America from his adopted home in France. He was on a lecture tour, on a plane to Seattle, sitting next to my father, seat 7-A.

The next day's *San Francisco Chronicle* carried his front-page story, headlined "A Private Talk with James Baldwin." In it, my father described the bestselling author, the wiry young man who grew up in Harlem the oldest of nine, who never knew his real father, who took the name of the man his mother married, a Pentecostal preacher with an ugly streak, and who at age fourteen started preaching himself, and then found respite, schooling, in books. Reading them and then writing them, starting with *Go Tell It on the Mountain* and *Giovanni's Room*.

My father called Baldwin "the most articulate essayist of the day, perhaps the most profound since Thomas Paine." Above the story was my father's byline: by William Hogan, literary editor.

"*Literary* editor," I can hear him saying. He would have drawn on a cigarette, inhaling deep into the unsettled caverns of his slouching torso. "Imagine that."

⊚

I am sure he never believed it. Never truly believed he had become literary editor of Northern California's largest newspaper. Gatekeeper to the West Coast's most important book market, "the most influential book critic west of New York," the newspaper proclaimed, a daily book columnist faithfully followed by hundreds of thousands of readers.

Like Baldwin, my father found respite from his past in the balm of books. But he never seemed to find that passionate knowledge of what a human being can do and, self-assured, become. It was as if he had to pinch himself, even as he lunched with Truman Capote at the English Grill in the St. Francis Hotel; clinked bourbon glasses with Carl Sandburg; attended Robert Frost's birthday luncheon; sat on the Pulitzer Prize jury that unanimously put Annie Dillard's *Pilgrim at Tinker Creek* forward for the 1975 nonfiction prize.

I am sure he thought that some prankster god had sprinkled him with literary fairy dust, that he simply appeared one day at that desk in the newspaper's book department, the desk where he would take calls from, write daily columns about, and correspond with most of the literary lights, publishing moguls included, of the mid-twentieth century. If newspaper pages were book leaves, my father would have written dozens of volumes. His characters would have included fiction writers like John

O'Hara, William Saroyan, Jessamyn West, Kurt Vonnegut, Philip Roth, Gore Vidal; nonfiction writers like Rachel Carson, Joan Didion, Janet Flanner, Norman Mailer; poets like Sandburg, the Beats, Archibald MacLeish, W. H. Auden; the names could fill a small ocean.

In my father's imagination, at least, the magic dust could wear off any time, and in a sparrow's blink, the prankster god would vanish, and he would be exposed, in front of millions of readers and fans, for the *poseur* he believed he truly was. The kid from Oakland who didn't go to UC Berkeley, because his family wouldn't support him studying anything but God or Banking. The book editor mortified by his own subpar spelling, his lack of formal literary training; ashamed he had never read *Ulysses* all the way through, that he didn't get to *War and Peace* until he was a corporal gunner in the 752nd Tank Battalion during the Second World War.

My father physically deflated, the balloon leaking helium, when a letter from some Stanford or Berkeley professor arrived on his desk to correct one of his columns. In a naked second, he would be transported back to the depths of the Great Depression, those nights that he heard his mother uttering novenas to *Saint Jude, Holy Saint Jude, Apostle and Martyr, great in virtue and rich in miracles, near kinsman of Jesus Christ, faithful intercessor of all who invoke thy special patronage in time of need.* Suddenly he would be back at the corner of Fifteenth and Telegraph in Oakland, trapped in the psyche of a young man who would never let him go.

Fifteenth & Telegraph

FROM MY FATHER'S NOTEBOOKS

In front of a shoe store there. It was 1935. I remember my shoes weren't very good. I thought, there has to be something more, some redemptive story behind this grotesque & depressing moment. Twenty-one and no job, no education to speak of, a family breaking up, a remnant of the middle class, disintegrating. And no one to talk to. Certainly not your bewildered, defeated parents.

I was embarrassed, even sore, that I wasn't at UC Berkeley where a lot of my friends were. But I was reading in those days, in the Oakland Public Library, as Jack London had. Feeling guilty about that because I wasn't working. Some minor—and major—moments came later. But I always had Fifteenth & Telegraph to measure them by.

My father always said my brother and I grew up in front of the massive brick fireplace in the center of my parents' house, the spot where we spent hours playing checkers, reading, building with Lincoln Logs, drying off after nighttime baths. As my father grew older, after he retired from the *Chronicle*, he often sat in the black leather chair in front of the fireplace and remembered, Palermo, Mondello, the war, the newspaper days, our childhoods, the good smells of pine and tar, the promise of things. I often came to visit him from my home across the bay in Oakland. On those foggy weekend afternoons he would start the fire early. Driftwood burns fast. I came to love the rich dusky-smoke smell, the creosote. It smells like the ocean, like the fireplace of our childhood, like my father. Those nights we would sit in the glow of the dwindling flames, and talk. After a few glasses of wine, my father would step down into the deep-worn grooves of reverie, the stories he told again and again, but always, somehow, at least in his mind, for the first time.

"The '30s weren't all bad, of course," he said on one of those nights. "In fact, that year, 1935, that dreadful year, was also the year I met Steinbeck. Have I told you about meeting Steinbeck in Monterey?"

He had, many times.

"No," I said. "What happened?"

"I was on a steam schooner that took me down to Monterey. She was putting in lumber there. I'd heard about a little literary magazine [the *Monterey Beacon*] in New Monterey on the mesa above Cannery Row. Published by a young fellow named Peter O'Crotty. An amateurish, if interesting, butcher-paper monthly. With radical linoleum cuts. I was interested in writing for it, even for no pay. Eventually did."

He got up, ambled out to the woodshed in the carport to

retrieve more driftwood. When he tossed it onto the embers, the wood sputtered, the flames shot high, sometimes curling, licking out onto the brick. Not frightening, just familiar.

"Look out, Daddy," I would say. "Your flame's out of control."

He would pour another glass of wine, ease back down into the chair, and by then, the flame had evened down. And the story continued, parts of which I remember from my childhood, long before I ever knew who John Steinbeck was.

"I went to see this O'Crotty and his girlfriend, the money lady. The girl, I forget her name, had a small horse ranch there. They told us that John Steinbeck, a writer who lived nearby and who'd just had his first success, a novel called *Tortilla Flat*, was writing for them. Steinbeck would give them stories for the loan of one of the horses. He loved to ride in the hills and forests above Monterey."

My father found out where Steinbeck lived, a modest bungalow in Tortilla Flat, then the Spanish paisano neighborhood. He paid a visit.

"I introduced myself as a 'writer.' But he couldn't have been more charming. Tall fellow, quiet yet talkative, who seemed genuinely interested in the young visitor, a 'writer,' for God's sake. His then-wife Carol had a WPA librarian's job. He was a full-time writer of fiction, a precarious occupation at any time. But, my God! In 1935?"

They survived, Steinbeck told my father. Steinbeck kept a skiff just down the hill at his friend Doc Ricketts's lab on Cannery Row. He gathered crabs and fished the bay. He said the lettuce truck from Salinas would cross over the Southern Pacific railroad tracks, and heads of lettuce would bounce off. He'd pick them up and take them home. Other trucks carried cabbage, artichokes, tomatoes—some days, armloads of tomatoes

Literary Thoughts

What books should a writer have to read? Hemingway presumed to answer that in one of his essays in the '30s (Esquire). Hemingway could be an awful wise-guy in his essays. Reading it again in a collection ... let's see: "War and Peace" and "Anna Karenina;" Flaubert's "Bovary" and "Sentimental Education;" Thos. Mann's "Buddenbrooks;" Joyce's "Portrait of the Artist," Ulysses;" "Tom Jones," "Joseph Andrews;" Stendhal's "The Red and the Black," "Huckleberry Finn"...

He goes on at some length—W. H. Hudson, Yeats, George Moore, de Maupassant, "The Brothers Karamazov," Stephen Crane, "The Portrait of a Lady," and other Henry James. I batted around .500 on all this.

I suppose it might help. It doesn't hurt to know the best of breed in any discipline. But I distrust lists ... I suspect that a Good Writer can be that without having read "Buddenbrooks," or others on H's list. If I were to make a list (which I won't) I might start with the "The Columbia Encyclopedia." And a half dozen really good books on the English Language, which unfortunately, I never mastered. And yes, a basic primer on spelling. And Captain Marryat, the English teller of Sea Tales, of course.

on the tracks, there for the taking. My father loved that story. He thought Steinbeck's freeloading cabbages and tomatoes was one of the great untold footnotes of Depression-era history, a story he should have written.

Steinbeck brewed a pot of tea. The two of them talked through the afternoon.

"He was always interested in people and what they were up to. When I left, he gave me a copy of an earlier novel, *To a God Unknown*, the British edition, because it hadn't been accepted for US publication. I have that book, autographed, by a future winner of the Nobel Prize in Literature."

That book is one of many of his I keep in a five-foot antique mahogany bookcase with beveled glass front and brass-key lock, built more than a century ago by Old Man Hugh, a relic that survived down the generations and, ever strange, managed to land in Palm Beach County, Florida.

"I remember that day," my father continued. "Where copies of the butcher-paper magazine are now, I have no idea. Maybe the Library of Congress."

I started to pour another glass of wine.

My father said, "Hold it there—I don't want you to get loaded, now. Remember, you have to drive back across the bay."

"I know, Daddy. I know."

The news story announcing my father's new post to the book desk described him as "unassuming, quiet, and capable," a veteran journalist who had served on the copydesk for the newspaper's Sunday-magazine section, had written for the section, had been drama editor for several years before, had been promoted to news editor of the Mediterranean editions of the

Influences

FROM MY FATHER'S NOTEBOOKS

*Well, Mencken, certainly. "The Story of Philosophy";
Hemingway, Dos Passos, the earlier Steinbeck. "The Boys
in the Back Room," as Edmund Wilson dubbed them.
Oh—James M. Cain, O'Hara, Saroyan, Raymond Chandler.
Rarely the classics. I have yet to read "The Wasteland."
I did finish "War and Peace," mostly in bivouacs in North
Africa in 1943. Proust bores me. Flaubert was okay.
Conrad—marvelous. But I did miss the classics. I never
read Mary Ann's "Faerie Queene," for example.... I stayed
with the Cezannes, the Paul Klees of literature, not the
Rembrandts and Michelangelos.*

****Also an influence: G. Bernard Shaw. E. L. Doctorow's
"Ragtime," a goofball kind of historical fantasy, a series
of intertwining narratives. Read it first in 1975 when it
was just published, and again just now. Doctorow—an
underestimated writer of fiction, a kind of American
Matisse, in prose, let's say. (Oh dear ... I would make a
very bad teacher of critical writing.)*

Stars and Stripes, the US Army newspaper, during the Second World War. If he weren't a literary editor, the newspaper said, "he'd probably be a sea captain. In fact, Hogan's idea of an absolutely perfect vacation is to get aboard a freighter going anyplace. Need it be added that eighty percent of the luggage he carries aboard is books."

I found my father's maiden column among hundreds of others in the basement library of the *Chronicle*, where I had made a pilgrimage to research his career. I was not at all surprised to find that his September 1955 "Greeting from the New Book Editor" humble, apologetic, almost, in describing who he was to be taking over the book pages from the late Joseph Henry Jackson, the *Chronicle*'s famous "Bookman."

My father wrote:

> *It was with some trepidation, that I,*
> *a kind of average "Man in the Gray*
> *Flannel Suit," agreed to move from the*
> *drama department into Joe's relaxed and*
> *friendly office. I believe he would have*
> *agreed that the person to do it should*
> *not be (as he never was) a "lit'ry" fellow;*
> *a member of any separate "school."*
>
> *Chiefly, Joe was always a top reporter in*
> *his field, a man who could communicate*
> *an idea instead of obscuring it through*
> *some showy display of intellectualism, or*
> *with snob prejudices. Whatever else Joe*
> *had, he had respect for the field he covered.*
> *And that's where I begin.*

Not long after, a phone call came to him at the newspaper. Said the voice: "Hello, my name is Kurt Vonnegut. I'm a writer." My father said: "You certainly are."

People always said my father was a different breed. He championed the good, the small, the unsung but worthy. So many good books were there for the reading, he wanted readers to know about them, like the Good News Radio Station he often joked about. Good things about good books. His readers didn't open the morning paper to hear rants from someone who had the power to rant. He never saw himself as a Titan who killed books at whim. That set him apart, brought him rabid professional associates, grateful fans.

He didn't just write about the well-known authors, the burgeoning talents, the rediscovered classics. He wrote about the culture of reading. The small presses. The Thoreau Society's pique at the excavation of the shores of Walden Pond. The Aid to the Visually Handicapped producing more than fourteen thousand large-print books for partially sighted children. A series of discussions by the Great Books Foundation, open to everyone, free of charge, at the public library.

When poet-bookseller Lawrence Ferlinghetti and one of his clerks were arrested for selling Allen Ginsberg's *Howl and Other Poems*, which Customs officials deemed "obscene," my father publicly thanked the San Francisco Collector of Customs for seizing *Howl*, thereby placing it on everyone's must-read list.

Dear Mr. Hogan:

I have just received word that SERMONS AND SODA-WATER is Number 1 best-seller in San Francisco, and I know whom to thank.

So I thank him.

14 Jan 61

Faithfully,

John O'Hara

William Hogan, Esq.

"It would have taken years," he wrote, "for critics to accomplish what the good collector did in a day." And as the convicted robber-rapist Caryl Chessman sat on San Quentin's death row for six years, writing four bestselling books by smuggling the manuscripts out of the prison, my father joined with intellectuals and artists, Norman Mailer to Pablo Casals to Robert Frost, demanding, in print, in letters to the governor, a stay of execution. Their message: keep him locked away in a 4.5-by-10.5-foot cell for the rest of his natural life, but for God's sake, let the man use a typewriter. He can write, they argued. But they argued in vain. Chessman's literary redemption ended May 2, 1960, in the San Quentin State Prison gas chamber.

My favorite story from my father's years as the *Chronicle*'s book editor, the one most keenly defining him: in January 1968 he boarded a Coast Guard cutter, the *Dexter*, with a crew of reservists and a load of books to deliver to the Good Neighbor Bilingual Public Library in La Paz, Baja California. The *Chronicle*'s news story about his trip ran under the headline "Literary Cargo."

⌃ John O'Hara, one of America's most prolific short story writers, says thanks, from my father's personal papers

It's my favorite because the story *is* my father. I can hear him say, "Put me on a ship heading out to sea, nothing to do but read, listen to the churn of the water, the gulls, and their cries. *Ahh.* The time, the place, and the girl."

I never saw the letters while he was alive.

He left them in a cardboard box in his backyard studio. No particular order, neither by date nor correspondent. When I took them back home, which was then Virginia, my husband placed them in large museum-quality binders, plastic leaves protecting them from decay. Every so often, I read over them. Each time I do, I again feel awe, an odd privilege, maybe, at finding myself an unintended party to a clutch of insider communiqués, intimate, chatty, a world behind a world behind a world. Many are typed, tumbling thoughts with the random rogue capital *G* or *C* poking above the line, the ink-filled *s*'s and *a*'s signaling the need for a new typewriter ribbon. Some include quirky return addresses at the top, like Owl Farm, Woody Creek, Colorado; Pretty Brook Road, Princeton, New Jersey; R.D. 2. QUOGUE, Long Island, N.Y., or just an elegant hotel name, The Warwick.

Other letters are written in gracefully measured hand-written script, the way grandmothers and schoolmarms once wrote. Some are scrawled, furious loops and dashes, the words decipherable only through patience. Many from authors are on plain light-brown copy paper, corrections and changes in ink, marked with carats on the typewritten text. Most of the letters from publishers are pristine, on bond stationery or note card, embossed heading, perfect type, no scratched-in corrections.

As a whole, the letters display a half-century parade of authors, editors, and publishers. They considered my father a colleague, an equal, maybe even better, a sounding board for news, fragments, and footnotes from literary history, priceless odds and ends that may not have appeared in any book, in any library anywhere. The letters are a brew of news and confidences from the authors' writing lives. The novelist Jack Kerouac, for example, described his upcoming novel *On the Road*. "I would like it to be the sendoff to a brand new American Literature of grand Goethean-Dostoevskyan confession," Kerouac wrote, "so we could have something to read in our old age that would be just too rich to fit into journalism & filmed drama, that is, books as books ... More simply, ON THE ROAD is just a tale of what happened told by a guy in a cafeteria."

I love that letter, the feel of it, two pages of galloping thoughts, of history spattered with phrases like "hepcats, bop, girls, kicks, visions, poets, Dharma-bumming."

Some offered up unexpected slivers of past literary lives, like the note from the poet-novelist Vincent McHugh, who shared the same agent as William Faulkner. "I only saw Faulkner once," McHugh wrote. "He was coming out of Ben's office just as I got out of the elevator. He had the air of a woods animal in the city. He did not look at me. He moved softly and silently along the wall, a small man whose hair was like fur."

Others still displayed gratitude for kindnesses large or small, a hallmark of my father's literary life. The letter from the novelist Alex Haley recounted their meeting on a ship when Haley was still in the Coast Guard, long before *The Autobiography of Malcolm X*, years before *Roots*. "Never will forget how when I was here, still in the Coast Guard, struggling to sell now and then to sundry magazines," Haley said, "and somehow I met you, and the big, powerful book critic William Hogan couldn't have been more sincerely gracious, and interested in me, as if I had been some major author. Never will forget it. I do not wish to sound maudlin, which would embarrass us both, but it really did mean such a lot in the way of encouragement."

I have that letter framed on my office wall. I know my father was proud of that happenstance moment at sea, when a young Haley handed him some early manuscripts to read, and my father helped unearth a talent.

A few of the letters bespeak an intimacy, a link between kindred spirits, people who share a heritage, a language, an understanding: the note card from the novelist John Gregory Dunne, for example, who endured the same corrosive Catholic upbringing as my father, and who was married to the novelist-journalist Joan Didion: "I'm sorry I did not use St. Leo's," Dunne wrote, "but the copy editor at S&S pointed out that I had five (5!) minor characters named 'Leo' and insisted I change four of them; it's my favorite name. I think I know a Leo.... Joan remembers you. She still cannot believe, almost 20 years later, that you saw her. As she remembers, she just called you up and asked if she could come to see you. She says it was a true act of kindness that you did."

I treasure that letter as well. I like Dunne—"Always under-rated," my father often said. But also, because his wife, Didion, has been a lodestone in my own life as a journalist and beyond. Didion writes about where I am from. California. Not the docks and fog of San Francisco, but the dry agricultural swatch of territory a hundred and fifty miles northeast of us, hotter and drier than my territory, but still, part of the land we both loved and left. I read her work now, in my Florida home, and feel that same leap of gut she describes, the ache and thrill of coming in on a plane and seeing below the place of my birth, of hers, lying just ahead. I am transported home. I read that note from Dunne, and

Discovery

FROM MY FATHER'S NOTEBOOKS

Maybe 1933–'34. My old high school friend Frank Bandy said,
"Hey, have you read this guy Hemingway?" No. I couldn't
find him in the stacks. But had heard he'd been serialized in
the old Scribner's Magazine. Sure enough, I found, in bound
back copies of Scribners ('26–'27) and gobbled—that's the
word—"The Sun Also Rises," and later, "The Green Hills of
Africa." This was something nobody had ever told me about.
Later, something like that happened when I read Saroyan.
What that slap-happy Armenian did with words. "The Daring
Young Man on the Flying Trapeze." Wow—when you're 20.
I also found old bound copies of the American Mercury
(1920s) in the Oakland Library. Henry L. Mencken. Wow
(when you're 20). I was getting an education in spite of myself.

What did you do today, Billy?

"Oh, I read twelve 'Americana' columns and learned about
the preposterous religious rites of the deep south, about the
Boobs and Boosters, the ridiculous antics of Congress, and
Mencken's great enthusiasm, Joseph Conrad."

(But she never asked).

imagine Didion, so tiny, taking the grand *Chronicle* elevator up to my father's office, tremblingly introducing herself, hoping he would somehow find the time to talk about her first collection of magazine pieces, *Slouching Towards Bethlehem*. I pinch myself, look again to make sure the letter says what it does. And then it all washes over me, my father's life as a literary critic, a life among thinkers, hand extended to genius, and I wish more than anything he had told me about the letters, that I could talk to him about them—the confidences, characters and loopy scrawls, the stationery, the three-cent stamps, what he thought, how he felt, as he ran his hand over each one.

On one of the few occasions our mother took my brother and me to a local church, the Sunday-school teacher asked the children to sit in a circle and tell what our fathers did for a living.

She came to my brother, who was eight.

"My father is … *um*, I think he's a bookie."

"Well—" the teacher said, "*that's* certainly interesting."

"Yep," my brother said. "He reads a lot of books."

My father read a lot of books. He often said that Dos Passos made prose sound like Scott Joplin. He told us his real education began when he was nineteen or twenty and discovered H. L. Mencken, who like my father, was an inveterate religion thrasher. Someone once asked Mencken what he would do if he found himself standing at the Pearly Gates under the glaring gaze of St. Peter. He answered, "I would say, 'Gentlemen, I was wrong.'"

My father loved that story, told it often, because it captured Mencken's mordant wit, a quality he so admired in his fellow journalist's prose. The Bible he also never finished.

Writers

FROM MY FATHER'S NOTEBOOKS

The urge to be listened to, to preach? to assert? Express ego? To identify self. What is Self? Think of all the people who are writing. Letters ... stories ... books. I used to feel sorry for those who published with the vanity presses. Paid to get their stuff placed between covers. A Book! Grandma has published a book! *Sometimes they'd call me and ask to be reviewed. They were never reviewed. It was a racket, that kind of publishing. A shame.*

⌃ I wonder what my father would say about the explosion of indie books that would remake his world in the digital age.

Pepper Trees

FROM MY FATHER'S NOTEBOOKS

Are smells—aromas, scents—influences? I think not. Merely evoke a time, an emotion. Pine smoke (Carmel, the Sierra). Kelp. The hot smell of a ship's engine room. Certain cooking, steaming crabs, Christmas pudding. Lilac. Pepper trees. Haystacks. Newly-printed books. Wet grass in sandy soil. Like sounds. An inter-urban train in the late afternoon. Does the whine of a carpenter's saw on that same afternoon still evoke sadness? Color? No. Yet I always like blue. Blue, my mother said, was the Virgin Mary's color. I think Mary would smile at that.

"In and around," yes, but he could quote from it. From Job: "The old lion perishes for lack of prey, and the cubs of the lioness are scattered." Ecclesiastes: "A time to keep, and a time to throw away." Psalms: "You have turned for me my mourning into dancing." Genesis: "And the gathering together of the waters He called Sea."

"Literature!" my father would say. "That's what it is—literature! And anyone who tells you differently, who says it's somehow mixed up with that medieval voodoo nonsense my sorry platoon of a family believed in, should have his head examined."

He read the artists of the Harlem Renaissance; read Ernest J. Gaines and Carl Sandburg, both the poetry and the massive biography of Lincoln. We grew up knowing that Sandburg was the only American writer to ever win a Pulitzer Prize for biography and another for poetry. He read Hawthorne and Melville, and checked in with Dickens from time to time. He delighted in James Thurber, A. J. Liebling, Lillian Hellman, Lillian Ross, and all the other writers from the early *New Yorker* magazine era.

He loved reading about the sea. His greatest enthusiasm, like Mencken's, was Conrad. Everything Conrad wrote sat in his library and got reread in front of his fire.

He read *Hakluyt's Voyages*, "the condensed version," tales of the English explorer who gathered narrative accounts of "traffics" in the Age of Exploration.

He read Eugene Burdick, *The Blue of Capricorn,* especially, and I can only imagine that he was quietly haunted by the wind-polished beauty of Burdick's words "there is a place where the Pacific coldly smokes." Because Burdick's smoky Pacific was my father's ocean, too. And his dream was to say it in prose.

But he couldn't. Or, never believed he could, never thought he was good enough. He never quite found the words, even though his notebooks and cargo load of columns teem with words, syllables that stun, that ripple like poetry, that make you want to turn them over again and again, drink in, repeat.

⊚

Plenty of people over the years said my father should write a book. *Short Takes,* as one suggested, or any book, really. The novelist William Saroyan once told him in a note, "If you're got enough stories and sketches for a book, or a novel, will you tell me a little about it? And send the stuff to Bennett A. Cerf, Random House...."

An invitation, a suggestion, a moment or two when someone believed he could.

⊚

So he retreated into books. Reading them. Writing about them. Returning to his favorites, always a discovery. Reading released him from the frail moorings of his outer self and carried him to the stirring waters inside. When he read, he lived there for a time as Conrad, Burdick, and the others set down in words what my father knew only in daydreams.

Strange, but I don't remember my grandfather Will saying anything about the book columns, about my father's career at the *Chronicle,* the "Voice of the West." Never heard him say, "Great column about Thoreau, Bill." Why? I don't know. Maybe by that time my grandfather was too defeated to muster generosity. I do remember them talking about books, things my grandfather was reading, Carlyle stands out. I remember as a child hearing them discuss "the reign of terror." I knew Carlyle's name long before I knew who he was.

Short Stories

There might have been a short story a while back about St. Denis du Sig, 1943, the French priest who watched tanks and personnel carriers churn up the dust . . . Maybe he (I) could write a short story based on that. He had, way back, wanted to be a writer. (Imagine, introducing myself to John Steinbeck as "a writer!") But the fact is, he wasn't disciplined enough. He didn't want to practice. It's like wanting to be a piano player. He read. But he failed to practice.

Fairy Tales

*A fairy tale from his own childhood, "What the Moon Saw,"
by Hans Christian Andersen. Each night the moon appears
briefly between the chimney pots and tells a poor lad a
story—what it saw the night before, or earlier that night.
The story has remained with him for decades. It is in a
book [pictured above] inscribed by his father: "To Bill, on
his fifth birthday, from Dad." Thank you!*

My grandfather loved books, always did, always read. But he never complimented my father. Maybe that's where it begins. I am sure my grandfather's early promise, his native intelligence, Stanford, the professor he might have become had Old Man Hugh not ground him down—haunted my father. Made him feel—what? Responsible? Guilty? For what? Or just sad, because a professor would have been a better father? Maybe my father's uncritical praise for my stories—*Brilliant!*—was his way of trying to buoy me because no one buoyed him. Mystery.

ESCAPE

I keep filling in the brackets, peering into, moving around in the fractured lives of those who went before me. Knowing their yearnings, their deep disappointments, brings me back to the land I was born to—middle Northern California, circling San Francisco Bay, ending at the Pacific Ocean, next stop, the Orient. I imagine they saw the same tides I saw, and even better, breathed the same air I breathed, air chilled by summer fog. You see it rolling, slow at first, then a furious tumble over the coastal hills, dollops of whipped cream spilling out of the fog machine from somewhere beyond. Sometimes fingers of puffed white inch down crevices on Mount Tamalpais, the high point jutting up north of the bay, and soon the temperature might drop twenty degrees. From the docks at the Embarcadero, or the ferry slips of Oakland, my forebears could see that same mountain, a backdrop, as they watched the steam schooners of my father's dreams, his "poetry on water."

At the old docks they watched the unloading of tons of fir, trees that made their way by schooner down from the Columbia River at the Oregon-Washington border. Or redwood, the giant spirits sliced down from doghole inlets on the Mendocino coast. My forebears, such as they were, passed by the onetime copra docks my father told me so much about, the pungent smells, the foreign tramps unloading goods from island ports in the South Pacific. They walked by the foot of Sacramento Street where cargo boxes read, in both Chinese and English, "Product of Hong Kong," exotic Depression-era treasure chests filled with Christmas-tree ornaments, sewing-machine heads, rayon kimonos, poker-chip racks, balloon inflators, flower bulbs, and swordfish steaks. That cargo is all gone now, yet remains part of their history, part of mine, adrift out there between the *old* and the *very, very old.*

Somehow, these visions carry me home.

I feel attached again to places of my childhood. The dry-grass hills, maybe a half-mile hike behind our house, up where purple lupine, orange poppies, buttercups, sticky monkey, and baby-blue eyes dot the green and gold grass in spring and summer; acres of wildflowers, constellations of color spattering the ground, all the way from that hill to the coastal highway. I see my parents' back-yard garden, rimmed with rhododendron hedges, a leafy retreat, sometimes tomatoes in summer, fulsome rosemary sprawling down the patio, a thirty-foot pine tree we planted ourselves, once a three-inch slip in a milk carton filled with good clean dirt.

From the top of that garden, you can see Tamalpais, which the Native peoples supposedly called the Sleeping Lady. Because, if you look at it right, the outline of the mountain could be a princess lying on her back. You can make out her face and long neck, the rise of her breast, and the dip to her waist; hair tumbling down the western part of the mountain behind her. The garden was a good place to be, a landscape that held me in place for a while.

One night, they all came to me in a dream, a hazy half-waking vision, Old Man Hugh, my grandfather Will, my great-uncle Howard, my father. There was no movement, no color, just a static photograph, varying shades of black and white, each man set apart from the other, as if all four images had been torn from four different eras, four separate lifetimes, then pasted back together as one. On the left was the Old Man, an oval-shaped, faded black-and-white portrait, formal, the image I once found in a dusty civics book, *Greater Oakland, 1911*. Gray hair closely cropped, balding; dramatic swatch of a gray-white mustache, almost handlebar in length, shading a stern mouth; white starched collar above a dark jacket; impassive face, eyes fixed on self-reliance. He is the picture of the good of the Christian ethic; a man in and of his time, secure at the pinnacle of his power.

In softer black-and-white, a gentler image from a slightly later time, maybe the early 1920s, stood my grandfather Will, dashing, truly. A younger man, sporting a tweed three-piece suit with pocket watch; square jaw; thick hair combed evenly back, light brown then, years before it thinned and turned white. He stood against a backdrop of books looking content, jaunty, even, as if occupying just the right time and place—the place being a gracious hydrangea-draped home in Piedmont, the wealthy

Harbor

FROM MY FATHER'S NOTEBOOKS

Any place which affords good anchorage and a fairly safe station for ships, or in which ships can be sheltered by the land from wind and sea. Also called haven. It is not necessary that it be landlocked or absolutely safe for ships. It is enough that it affords a reasonably safe place for retreat from wind and storms.

—INTERNATIONAL MARITIME DICTIONARY

hilltop crescent above Oakland, where a flower-petal beauty of a wife hosted society teas and bridge games. A time when there was hope and promise, before he knew he was heir to something that would never be.

In the next panel over, close in proximity but separated by ragged, ripped photograph edges, came my great-uncle Howard. His image was sepia toned, with shades of meaning, echoes, mystery. He stood on a golf course, Scotland, I think, where he traveled for a medical fellowship in the 1930s. He smiled, captivated by something either inside himself, or in the enigmatic distance beyond the photograph. One hand was stuffed in his tweed jacket pocket, the other by his side, holding a cigarette. His strong, stockinged calves were visible below the tweed plus fours. Behind him were a few crooked trees and a barren hill. Yes, Scotland, the place he had fled to, to capture his dream.

In the final image, in clearer, newer, glossier black and white, stood my father. He leaned against the railing of a tanker he once boarded in the 1960s, bound for Hilo, Hawaii. A captain's hat covered his thick carpet of salt-and-pepper hair, always cut in a flattop. His dark-rimmed glasses slipped slightly down his nose. He held a cigarette out over the railing. He was smiling, not wide, he never smiled wide; more of a half smile. But clearly, happy, for he was on a ship bound for elsewhere. The waters of the Pacific stirred below him, and beyond.

What was the meaning? Why did all four men come to me in one vision, this strange mélange of photographs from my memory, side by side yet separate, each inhabiting his own world? I search for a sign, a fragment of meaning, if meaning is to be found. The Emerson piece I read at the Old Man's gravesite? "One blood rolls uninterruptedly an endless circulation through all men, as the water of the globe is all one sea, and, truly seen, its tide is one." A hint, maybe. A bracket.

talk of the town, streets of Oakland, 1923—

you hear? only took him a few seconds,
seemed like ... yeah, papers said just
five. how did he do it? ... i couldn't see ...
grown men pushing grown men out of the
way ... looked like a thousand people ...
heard someone yell, "ya should have your
will ready!" a hundred and twenty-two
feet in the air ... good god, it was terrific
... houdini! ... all that weight and rope
and upside down and such—and he was
still able to escape.

The newspaper said ten thousand people jammed Thirteenth Street, downtown, to watch the spectacle of Harry Houdini, heels pointed to the heavens, Harry Houdini, swinging in the wind by a rope, suspended from the ninth floor of the newest American skyscraper, the *Oakland Tribune* clock tower.

He was wrapped up in what was billed as an escape-proof outfit, a heavy straitjacket the police chief got up from the bowels of the jail and then spent five minutes locking shut, front to back, back to front, and front to back again. The chief tied him up tight with the same rope they used to hoist him up the side of the building.

Houdini dangled upside down above the dizzy throngs, swayed above men who left their work, women who left their mah-jongg games, boys who slipped out of school, they all came to see the spectacle. Harry Houdini, suspended, ten thousand people holding their breath. *One second ... five seconds ...* and then the heavy jacket dropped to the platform below, just missing the chief of police. Houdini waved his unbound hands.

Ten thousand cheers.

The Houdini escapade in Oakland was just one of hundreds of spectacles, stunts, diversions, fads, and impromptu parties taking place in cities across the nation during the 1920s, when the US government decreed, via the Eighteenth Amendment to the Constitution, that liquor was now illegal. A time when more young people chugged more alcohol, more hooch, more highballs and Manhattans, more straight-up gins and whiskeys, than they'd ever chugged before. F. Scott Fitzgerald knew this time, and wrote: "It was an age of miracles, it was an age of art, it was an age of excess, and it was an age of satire."

It was the age of my great-uncle Howard Hogan.

Howard Hogan, my grandfather's much younger brother, the Old Man's eighth child, unintended, an afterthought, "a mistake," as my father always said, was a child of the new century. A century of automobiles, psychology, of boundless new ideas, leaps in science and literature, an intellectual breakaway from the stifling industrial past.

Howard was a graduate of the United States Naval Academy, which was built in "secluded" Annapolis, the story goes, to save midshipmen from "the temptations and distractions" of big cities. An elaborate certificate of graduation, signed by President Warren G. Harding, hangs on a wall in the garage of my Palm Beach County, Florida, home. Like his older brother, Howard consumed books. He and my grandfather Will argued about

Homer, Plutarch, Freud, the Russian Revolution. Anything was possible in a dizzying world in delicious upheaval.

Howard was on his way to becoming a doctor when it happened.

◎

talk of the town, streets of Oakland, 1924—

you hear? jolson's coming to oakland—
greatest entertainer in the world. richest,
too ... al jolson i hear "california" all the
time, folks whistling it on the street car
... they say his new show ... "bombo," is
it? ... biggest ever, twenty songs at least
... he got thirty-seven curtain calls in new
york—in blackface ... he's a jew you know
... read somewhere, maybe scribners, he
was asa yoelson, son of a russian cantor.
they call him "jolie" ... imagine that—a
big shot entertainer coming to town.

◎

A sun-kissed miss said, "Don't be late!"
That's why I can hardly wait,
Open up that Golden Gate
California, here I come

◎

AL JOLSON COMES TO AUDITORIUM

June 1, 1924
Oakland Tribune

Al Jolson, unique and
inimitable entertainer, will
be seen for one performance
only, Monday night, June 2,
in the Oakland Auditorium
Theatre.

ⓢ

I have often imagined what was said between Howard and
his aging father, Old Man Hugh, the night of June 1, 1924, the
night before Al Jolson was to appear at the Oakland Auditorium,
the night it happened. It would have been around 7:00 p.m. when,
or if, they spoke.

Old Man Hugh: "You're going out?"

Howard: "Yes, Father. Motoring."

"Pastime of the Devil."

"No, Father, pastime of young men of means, humor, imagination, goodwill, and rare taste. For gin."

"Ah. Sarcasm. Send a boy for an education and he comes back
a smart-ass in a fancy suit."

"Or a uniform … remember, sir, 'What comes out of the mouth proceeds from the heart, and this is what defiles.' Goodnight, Father."

"Impudence. Work of the Devil."

If it actually had happened, what was the Old Man thinking?

Did he really mean it?

Did Howard fight back?

I see him peppering his father with words from the biblical prophet Malachi, as was his habit with friends, an intellectual game that earned him the nickname "Mal." *And he shall turn the heart of the fathers to the children, and the heart of the children to their fathers, lest I come and smite the earth.*

If it happened, did the Old Man know his son was laughing at him? Was he laughing back? He couldn't read, but he wasn't stupid.

"For the Old Man," my father once told me, "Howard was the big question mark. The question was 'why?' And on that night, I'm sure he thought, *why?*—why in God's name was this child of mine ever born?"

One thing I know for certain: unlike his older brother, Howard never withered under the sting of the Old Man's wishes. Never let the locust bore into him. Like Houdini, Howard escaped.

Whether my father escaped his ghosts depends on who's telling the story. I think he did. He escaped to the newsroom. He became a journalist over his family's objections. His mother called reporters "worthless drunks, rubbish who embarrass themselves by prying into other people's lives." In this she echoed the few elders who had not been ruined by the stock-market crash.

Influences (ships)

FROM MY FATHER'S NOTEBOOKS

It started with the ferry boats when I was very young.
The water. The wake. The screech of the ferry slips.
And what you saw from the decks, Goat Island, gulls,
Marine traffic, tugs, barges, the steam schooners, coastal
lines, the big ships. Then the lumber schooners in my
teens. That was one thing my father did for me—arranging
through his cousin to let me travel aboard the lumber
ships. Ships. An extension of dreams ... Vehicles of escape
... Escape from—what? A dismal, crumbling unimaginative
family, stuck in the past ... Ah, but then, the smells—copra,
coffee, a time when San Francisco was a world port and
Shanghai began at the bottom of Sacramento Street.
I just wanted to get aboard.

William Hogan, newspaperman, got a byline on a big city paper even though that "crumbling lot" he came from told him they wouldn't pay for college unless my father studied the priesthood—or maybe banking, which would lead to a proper job at the Bank of America, like the other young men from good families. My father never forgot it, the venom of it, his own father standing there, passive, gnarled, afraid to say a word, to stand up for his son, as the will of the family made itself known. Yes, my father escaped to the newsroom. But somewhere, in the deepest regions of his inner self, where the rivulets trickling through our private landscapes make us who we truly are, he never broke away.

Nathan Leopold and Richard Loeb, the two Chicago boys from money, lots, Sears, Roebuck money, escaped after they lured little Bobby Franks to their green Willys-Knight auto, and then, just for fun, slashed him with a chisel to the head before dumping his naked body—barely recognizable because of the hydrochloric acid they poured on him—into a culvert.

They got caught. But then, they escaped again. They escaped the noose.

Death by hanging. A form of capital punishment going back to biblical times. At first common in this country, hanging was soon abolished by all states but two as too cruel. Too many things could go awry. If the hangman's noose was too short, not thirteen turns but only five or six, the prisoner's neck wouldn't break. He would strangle to a slow death. If the rope had too much slack, the drop from the gallows platform would be too fast. The final jerk could snap a prisoner's head clean off.

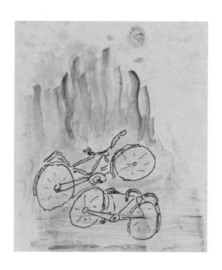

Fifteenth & Telegraph II

FROM MY FATHER'S NOTEBOOKS

He reflects again. 1935. My father? He simply couldn't make it. Had to sell the Ricardo Street house and move into some bum boarding house. My father, the well-dressed bum.

My mother, my sister and I moved back in with the grandparents. Will drifted to Los Angeles, probably hitching a ride on a train, or a truck. He hoped friends there would find him a job. He kept drifting. He would write me long typewritten letters, full of trivia and guilt, things he could have done, might have been. It was here that I got bored with him. Bored, then irritated with the position he had placed his wife and children in. Irritation gave way to—what? Anger? Apathy? Somewhere I had lost a father.

Leopold and Loeb escaped the noose because their defense attorney, Clarence Darrow, perhaps the most eloquent orator in this nation's legal history, convinced the judge, in a twelve-hour summation, that, yes, even though the crime was unspeakable—hydrochloric acid to try to erase a little boy—and, yes, even though the defendants were guilty (he had them plead so), Nathan Leopold and Richard Loeb, ages nineteen and eighteen, *just boys, Your Honor, just boys*, didn't deserve the noose.

From Darrow's summation, August 22, 1924:

> *Why did they kill little Bobby Franks?*
> *Not for money, not for spite; not for*
> *hate. They killed him as they might kill a*
> *spider or a fly, for the experience. They*
> *killed him because they were made that*
> *way. Because somewhere in the infinite*
> *processes that go to the making up of the*
> *boy or the man something slipped, and*
> *those unfortunate lads sit here hated,*
> *despised, outcasts, with the community*
> *shouting for their blood . . .*
>
> *I suppose civilization will survive if your*
> *Honor hangs them. But it will be a terrible*
> *blow that you shall deal. Your Honor will*
> *be turning back over the long, long road*
> *we have traveled.*

The facts of the case were not in dispute.
Only whether or not the young men were insane.

If my grandfather's stories are true, the singer-comedian Al Jolson, actually called by some "the greatest entertainer in the world," met and befriended Howard Hogan on the Oakland–San Francisco party circuit. Whenever Jolson toured the West Coast, he met up with Howard at the poshest speakeasies, the best parties hosted by the richest of Oakland's young set, the places where pretty girls showed up in silk drop-waist dresses, bows at the shoulder, dark-red lipstick, and rouge on their cheeks, sometimes on their knees. As a child, I didn't know who Al Jolson was, but I knew his name, heard it whenever people talked about Uncle Howard. "Someone was with him in the car that night," my grandfather said, many times. "It was Al Jolson, Jolson, the most famous entertainer in the world." The name "Jolson" entered the family mythology, as real to us as grandmother Mildred's beaded wedding dress.

What happened later that night, I often wonder, after Howard and the Old Man's talk? In my mind's eye I see Jolson, the great entertainer, and Howard, Old Man Hugh's youngest son, standing on the top deck of the ferry on a night crossing from San Francisco back to Oakland. They drank gin from a silver flask carved with Howard's initials. Maybe they hummed, "California here I come, right back where I started from," passing the flask, drinking the gin—singing now—"O-pen up your Gol-den Gate … Cal-i-for-nia, here I come." Howard's automobile, a new red Lincoln touring car, sparkling headlights popping out like oversized bug's eyes, silver hood ornament polished to a shine, sharp as unused cutlery, spare tire, red to the rim, secured to the running board just in front of the driver's door—that car sat below deck where autos go for the ride. "Jolie" Jolson and Howard Hogan, coming back from a party in San Francisco, always a party in San Francisco, always another place to go when the ferry docked on the other side.

The real story, the whole story, twists and groans as it emerges, half a step ahead or behind at any moment. The truth, if there is one, is born of both the fluid—things we see, remember, create, imagine—and the immutable, that which we can objectively measure. The fluid is always changing, ever a question. The look on a man's face, for example, or how a summer night smelled. Whether guests had a fine time at the party, whether or not they drank too much. Even how the world came into being. These will surely differ with the telling.

Is what my grandfather told me the real story? Is what I tell you the truth? Judges and juries, also journalists, decide such things every day. That's why we love immutable facts. How many beads on the wedding dress? Today's exact price, in dollars per hundred square feet, of a load of redwood. Objective. Measurable.

For the judges, juries, and journalists who tell us what is so, the real story, or at least the day's rough-hewn version of it, emerges only after the fluid and immutable meet in the middle, wave hitting rock, to mix, bounce off, or bind to one another.

Some of the fluid parts to the story of the night of June 1, 1924, in Oakland, California:

At 11:45 p.m., more or less, witnesses heard either a "thump" or a "crash."

Just before that, people on East Twelfth Street and in a nearby restaurant saw a "large car" speeding by. They could not agree on whether the car sped past another going in the same direction. Some said the car was going sixty miles per hour. One said seventy. A man who got out of the car after it stopped said twenty-five.

One person saw the car go by with its top down. Three people were inside, he said, one of them in the back seat, leaning forward, almost touching the driver's seat. Another saw more than one person in the car, two, maybe, but maybe more, one of them "definitely" a woman.

Reflection

Why is he doing this (he asked himself one evening?)
These jottings, these notes ... Raw material? But for what?
Perhaps Mary Ann might pick up a line here or there to
work in somewhere. There was a short story a while back,
wasn't there? Some figures whose lives are so intriguing
inspire several biographies. Tsarina Catherine, Freud,
Tolstoy, Hemingway. Howard Hogan? Uncle Howard.
Now there might be a story—the only interesting character
from that miserable Oakland clan I've spent my life trying
to shake. Fascinating character, really. Good God.

Others saw the car go by with the top up, one person inside, a man in a light-colored suit and straw hat. Still another saw a second man get out of the car after it stopped, wearing a suit "bordering on the flashy." Others saw two men dressed in dark clothes exit the car doors, one of them disappearing into the dark.

According to one witness, a man who stepped out of the car after the crash smelled of wine or, maybe, whiskey. Another witness said that man staggered alongside the car after he got out "appearing intoxicated." A police officer reported that the man who stepped out of the car was not intoxicated, did not smell like liquor. Another police officer said the man who stepped out of the car said, "I'm responsible. And I'm ready to take my medicine."

All witnesses seemed to agree that after the thump, or crash, the car traveled for another 175 feet. All agreed that, as the car went that final distance, two bodies were pinned to the hood.

Some of the immutable facts from that same Sunday night, June 1, 1924: two men, a D. R. Rogers and a George Rogers, were hit by a speeding car. The speeding car was a shiny new red Lincoln touring car. The victims, business partners at an Oakland auto body shop, were not related. Both were immigrants from Mexico. Both had changed their names from "Rodriguez" to "Rogers."

Both men had so many broken bones their bodies looked like rag dolls.

Both men were dead.

After the crash, one man stood alone outside the car. The man who stood alone outside the car ran to the victims, tried to carry one of them to another car parked by the curb, telling police he had to "get these men to the emergency hospital."

No one would help him.

A crowd gathered at the scene of the crash, shouting, "Lynch him! Lynch him!"

Police arrested the lone man, handcuffed him, placed him in a police car, drove him away.

The next day's *Oakland Tribune* carried a front-page story with the headline:

TWO KILLED BY ANNAPOLIS GRAD'S AUTOMOBILE

Howard Hogan, Son of Wealthy Lumberman, Arrested after Fatal Accident

The same day's paper carried a story, back on page fifteen, with the headline:

AL JOLSON ABANDONS POPULAR SHOW

Comedian Secretly Boards Train for East after Disagreement; Leaves Note: "I'm Through"

EYE OF THE STORM

Palm Beach County, Florida, October 24, 2005, day of the hurricane

The eye of the storm. You hear the phrase, read it, people use it to describe a moment of meaning, an awareness of what's befallen them. But it's just words. Words you can't really know until the eye itself hangs over you, hovers, a massive spaceship of eerie stillness over the 2,386-square-mile expanse of the county.

Thirty miles just to the north of us live some of the wealthiest people in the world, at last count, forty-three billionaires, entrepreneurs, sports heroes. The same distance to the west, you enter the Glades, home to some of the poorest people in America, workers in the sugarcane fields, who pick the cane that goes to the refineries making Florida sugar kings rich, twelve hours of picking before they go back to their shacks of scavenged aluminum to cook the beans they got from a food bank in town to feed their six children, boys and girls who will one day be old enough to work in the sugar fields, too.

I won't remember how long we are in the eye of the hurricane. I will remember people coming out of their houses. Greeting neighbors. Walking dogs. Children running, parents in hip boots following, studying fallen-down trees, those that gave up the fight and tumbled over in leafless defeat. People talking on cell phones. Telling friends and family they are alive, houses intact. That we are under the eye now, and would be for—how long? An hour? Fifteen minutes? When we all go back inside, when the eye passes, we will be hit not by winds from the north or the south or the east, but by all of them together, all at the same time, the Trumps, Tiger Woods, the people who pick the sugar, all sides now, winds to smash the aluminum shacks of the people in the Glades to send their couches and pillows flying onto the streets where they will sit for weeks, all at once, the wind, the couches, the shacks, the furious trees, because that's what it means to live in Palm Beach County, Florida, under the eye of the storm.

◎

talk of the town, Oakland, California,
October 27, 1924—

you hear about the hogan trial? ... to think
the old gent had a son like this ... rich kid
drunk in a fancy car ... you crazy? howard
hogan is innocent, no way he did it ... the
newspapers are on it like locusts ... wasn't
a seat in the courthouse ... should have
sold tickets to get in there ... the district
attorney is trying it himself ... it does look
like the kid did it ...

The trial of the *People of the State of California v. Howard Francis Hogan* began on a soggy Monday. The charge, manslaughter. On the night of June 1, the People alleged, Howard Hogan, age twenty-three, youngest son of one of Oakland's wealthiest, most prominent citizens, ran down and killed two men, two auto-body workers out for a late-night stroll, Hogan in his shiny new Lincoln, a machine he drove at high speed after liquoring himself up to a sleepwalk.

The rain turned the packed courtroom to a swelter. Half the city of Oakland, it seemed—carpenters and plumbers, Knights of Columbus officers, wharf men, business owners, their wives—had waited since six in the morning in a line that snaked around the courthouse, hoping for a chance at a seat inside. In the front row sat the defendant's father, Old Man Hugh, nearing age seventy. Next to him, Hugh's wife, Anna, one of their daughters, and their oldest son, my grandfather Will, age forty-two. A special table at left, across from the jury box, was set aside for the press. Present that day, and throughout the trial, were reporters from the *Oakland Tribune, San Francisco Examiner, San Francisco Chronicle,* other city papers, the *News,* the *Call,* and the *Bulletin,* as well as papers from up and down the state. The presiding judge, Fred V. Wood, had his hands full in the case of *California v. Hogan,* a matter unlike any other that had appeared before him, a society drunk-driving manslaughter case, perhaps the first in a California courtroom.

The papers didn't say, but I imagine Old Man Hugh was not only pained by the spectacle, but shamed. Just a year earlier, he had addressed a group of seven hundred civic men, among them some of those same lawyers, the judge himself, all gathered at a white-tie banquet to celebrate Oakland's progress. The event was splashed over two full pages in the next evening's *Tribune.* Now, each day of the trial, the front page of that same newspaper described him as "Hugh Hogan, wealthy lumberman, father of the defendant, Howard Hogan, driver of the death machine."

Palm Beach County, Florida, day of the storm

My sons and I are sitting on the living-room couch. My husband is in the bedroom. Listening to the hand-crank radio. Governor Bush has declared a state of emergency. He spoke to the president, his brother, by phone this morning, asking for federal help. They will bring in the National Guard.

My heart is pounding.

"This is intense," says William, my almost-sixteen-year-old.

I am not crying. I don't want to scare my child.

His heart is pounding, I can hear it in his voice, see it in his eyes.

When I think back, it seems strange, but there were no flying thoughts, no hurricanes in the head, no quicksand in the arms, no swirling thoughts as the eye passed and the wrath of the storm exploded. What might have once been thoughts in the head, my head, streaking thoughts, are now so real, surreal, so full of fury, there are no words to bring meaning. The meaning, the words, won't come, there are no thoughts. Only my shaking hands, pushing buttons on my cell phone to call my brother in California.

"I have to talk to you."

I move to the pantry where my son can't hear me. I can cry now.

"You have to promise me," I say.

"Of course, anything," he says.

"Promise me that if I die, you'll come to get me, and bring me back home, and you'll scatter my ashes at the driftwood beach."

"Oh, sweetie, you're not going to die."

"You have to promise you'll scatter me there so I can be with Mom and Daddy."

But I can't hear him anymore. The crashing is too loud. There is flying landscape, just outside my window. Trees, a bicycle someone forgot to bring in, a mailbox, stray pieces of aluminum shuttering, acres of branches, barrel roof tiles, landscape overturned, upended, streaking past, more than the mind can drink in. Hearts are pounding. Nobody is crying. We are waiting. My cat, Katie, is somewhere in the house hiding, trying to feel safe, like her feline ancestors who hunkered down in fallen carved-out trees.

My twelve-year-old son James mercifully sleeps.

Oakland, California, 1924

The manslaughter trial of *California v. Hogan* lasted eleven days. During that time, Old Man Hugh, his wife, Anna, and their son, my grandfather Will, sat listening to witnesses tell of illegal liquor consumed or not consumed, of parties attended or not attended, of companions in the car or not in the car the day of June 1, the day leading up to that night when the "death machine," the shiny red Lincoln touring car registered in Howard Hogan's name, slammed into and killed two men.

The defense hoped to show that Howard wasn't drunk that night, that the event was "a horrible, unavoidable accident" that took place on a darkened street, no moon, no lights, when the two victims happened to step out of nowhere, into the path of the car.

"We will show," the lead defense attorney told the court, "that ... Hogan attempted to apply his brakes. That he doesn't remember what happened for a few seconds after. He was in shock. That he brought his car to a stop as quickly as possible. We will show that he then jumped out of the car, and ran back to the men who were injured. We will show that his sole and only effort was to get these men to a place where they could receive medical assistance."

For the prosecution, the district attorney said they would prove that the defendant was drunk, out of control, a "wanton youth of privilege out for a joyride."

Reporters hung on every word.

"We will show," the district attorney said, "that the defendant, Howard Hogan, was under the influence of intoxicating liquor, and was driving on the left-hand side of the road, between seventy and eighty miles an hour, when this tragic accident occurred."

Officer Gallagher testified that, when Howard Hogan was arrested, "he talked in a gentlemanly manner."

"What did he say?" the attorney asked.

"He said he was ready to take his medicine."

"Did the defendant smell like liquor?"

"No, he did not. He did not smell like liquor."

There was a bachelor party the afternoon of the accident, other witnesses said, where Howard Hogan might have been drinking "a highball or another such concoction." He was not seen drinking anything else at the party.

After the party, the host testified, four men, he and Howard among them, joined four young women and drove off, two cars, for supper.

"Did you know the women?"

"They are prominently known in San Francisco, and I don't want to give their names."

The witness wasn't pressed further.

The jury listened as witnesses told of Howard returning from San Francisco and driving to Toyans, a speakeasy just out of town. He was not seen drinking alcohol at the club. He was with two men and a woman. The woman and Howard Hogan had a fight, "a lover's spat," according to a defense witness. The woman left, angry. Howard Hogan followed. But another woman, or maybe the same woman, it wasn't clear, appeared at the club later on. Someone was driving Howard Hogan's car. The defense talked about producing "a mystery witness," someone else in the car. Two people, maybe. A man and a woman, in the car. The mystery witness never appeared. The name was never revealed. One witness testified that a "man got out of the car after the crash wearing a suit bordering on the flashy." Another car might have driven away.

"He was drunk," one witness said. "I smelled either wine or whisky on his breath, so strong it was sickening."

"Why do you say 'either wine or whisky'?" the attorney asked.

"I don't know."

As a child, I remember my grandfather Will talking about the trial, a grand circus of an event, women in fine dresses, men in hats, so many people in the room the judge kept calling, "Order! Order!"

My grandfather always said that Howard, his baby brother and confidant, was not driving the car that night. He always said two companions were with him: Al Jolson, "the most famous entertainer in the world," and a young woman, a San Francisco society belle. That either Jolson or the girl was driving along East Twelfth Street when the victims stepped into their path. He always said that Howard took the blame, protected his friends, shielded the girl from certain infamy, and saved Al Jolson's career.

Were my grandfather's stories true?

He would not say how he knew what he knew. Perhaps Howard shared a secret only with his big brother.

Were the newspaper stories true? Or just evidence of the search for truth?

"Hogan's recital on the witness stand of his version of the accident was dramatic," the *Oakland Tribune* said. "The largest crowd that has attended any court session of the trial was on hand to hear the defendant's story. Hogan spoke in a clear, firm voice and did not lose self-control, except on one occasion, when he was telling of the threats made against him by those in the crowd."

The paper said that Howard Hogan dropped his head, face flushed. That he stammered over the word "hang," or "lynch" when he described the crowd calling for his head in a noose. Then he gathered his composure. The story continued.

"What did you do immediately after the impact?" the prosecutor asked.

"I just sat there."

"You didn't do anything else?"

"I couldn't."

"You didn't see any form on your car, on the front of it after the impact?

"No."

"You lost your mind so completely you didn't know whether there were one, two or three people there?"

"I didn't lose my mind. I knew what was going on. I was stunned."

The defense attorney asked if anyone else was in the car. Howard Hogan looked at his attorney, then over toward the jury box. There, he fixed his eyes.

He paused. He said: "I was absolutely alone."

Palm Beach County, Florida, the day after the storm

We are alive. We did not die at the hands of a five-hundred-pound gas barbecue. Trees are felled across streets, across wide Palm Beach County boulevards. There are no traffic lights. People die in traffic accidents. More people die in traffic accidents after the storm than die during the storm. Walgreens around the corner has put out a sign offering free twelve-packs of water to any family who wants one, "no purchase necessary." The jungle behind our house has turned to a mass of naked tree trunks. Firewood for our patio fire bowl.

A sign in our neighborhood in front of someone's house: "Free Hot Coffee." We are without power. Friends and family overnight us food, steaks, fresh bread, fruit. The US Postal Service comes through. We share the bounty with neighbors. They share with us. Ten days without power, ten nights communing with neighbors, some we had never met before, sharing food and stories of the storm around each other's barbecues.

The sewers have backed up. Sewage burbles from the grates onto the street. We go to Walgreens to buy Clorox to pour over the grates. We come home with a free twelve-pack of water. We read later in business journals that orange-juice futures reached the highest level in six years just a few days before the storm, closing up 2.9 cents at $1.118 per pound.

My husband makes me coffee in the morning on the gas barbecue. I smell it when I wake up. My birds have come back. They now land on the giant toothpick tree trunks, the place that once was our jungle. They sing as if nothing has happened, dive-bomb into the pond, as if there had been no eye of the storm. They still come up with Florida fish in their beaks.

It is hot today. No air-conditioning. The newspaper says a cold front is coming. A giant tree has crashed the entrance gate to our community. The tumbled tree, an act of God, has crashed the gate, and now we can come and go. I am free to go.

My garden is strewn with branches. My orange tree still stands. With the help of my sons, I return my mother's pelicans, my father's driftwood, to the garden. My tomatoes are scattered to the heavens. My cat, Katie, lies in the sun. My husband makes me more coffee. A neighbor brings us bread.

People are out taking videos. The newspapers assess the damage. We read the Glades suffers more than we do. In the Glades, there is only strewn life, picked-apart life. The children who will one day work in the sugar fields need water to drink. There is no water. The state sits on water, is surrounded on three sides by water, but there is no water. They are in need of blankets because their beds and couches have been strewn across the streets of the Glades, a place that now looks like the garbage dump where my father used to haul debris, old boxes, planters, toys, broken things. The seagulls would come to the dump to scavenge my father's tossed remnants. The seagulls come to the Glades to scavenge from the people whose couches are scattered like seeds.

My palm trees are haggard, shorn, but not downed. Native palms, I find out, are built to bend and sway with the winds. If they do tumble, their roots regenerate, and they bounce back, a miracle of nature. My children lie on their backs at night on the trampoline and watch the stars. There are no streetlights. On those nights the stars are so bright, as new to them, as I imagine, those same stars were in the beginning.

Oakland, California, November 20, 1924, 5:00 p.m.

"Ladies and gentlemen of the jury, have you reached your verdict?"

They all sat waiting, the newspapermen, the judge, the spectators in their hats, the families of the victims, the working men, the wealthy, waiting to hear the outcome of the spectacle of *California v. Hogan*. My great-grandfather, great-grandmother, my grandfather Will, others, a cousin, an uncle, all in the front row still. I imagine the Old Man's eyes stern, fixed. But where? On the jury? On his son at the defendant's table? I imagine the Old Man's wife, the patient Anna, closing her eyes, and with trembling hands, making the sign of the cross.

"We have, Your Honor."

I imagine my grandfather Will clenching his teeth, wishing more than anything he believed in God just then, believed in the power of the sign of the cross, in some power greater than himself. I wonder whether he stared at his baby brother Howard, at the jury, at the foreman. The papers didn't say whether Howard looked down, out at his family, his brother, whether his eyes were open or shut. In my imagination, he was looking off, just beyond it all, captivated by something either inside himself, or just outside the frame.

The courtroom spectators waited to hear the end of the story, for the one word, or the two, that would alter a young man's life. The newspapers said that after the verdict, the defendant's father "comforted the defendant's mother, who seemed unable to leave her chair." That the defendant Howard Hogan stood in the middle of the courtroom, alone, while members of his defense team stood off to the side of the courtroom talking. That members of the jury "refused to discuss the case with representatives of the press." That "all inquiries were referred to the foreman." That the jury, for a time, had appeared deadlocked. That one of the jurors, a Mrs. Spencer, was overheard to say, "We fought against this thing with everything we had." That as the verdict was read, two of the women jurors could be seen crying.

I wonder what my grandfather Will looked like when the verdict was read. Whose hand he clasped; which juror's eye he caught, whose outstretched arm he grabbed. Whether he, too, along with the Old Man, embraced the patient Anna, the defendant's mother, his mother, as the foreman of the jury uttered: "Guilty."

Palm Beach County, Florida, five days after the storm

I drive across town to a nature preserve on the Atlantic coast, six miles as the egret flies from our home. I am not a nature buff, but somehow, I need to go, to understand what we just survived. Strange. The first time since our move from California to Virginia, from Virginia to Florida, that I feel compelled to go anywhere, and it is to walk through the shredded heart of the place that is now my home.

The preserve is a litter heap of branches, downed ficuses, crashed strangler figs, acres of tangle of a onetime forest. A naturalist explains that even though the place might look like a tree cemetery, it is anything but. It is, rather, a new place, a new coastal Eden, regenerating, being birthed in front of our eyes. During a hurricane, he says, creatures, trees, even humans, transcend. They become stronger, if that's what they are meant to do, if that is nature's intent.

No person, the naturalist tells us, manages his affairs as well as a tree does.

Tiny shoots that had been in the shadow of the large felled trees are already starting to come back. My garden will grow again.

NAUTILUS

San Quentin State Prison, Marin County, California. The name evokes infamous lodgers: the Old West outlaw Black Bart, the bigamist wife killer "Blue Beard" Watson, the cultist mass murderer Charles Manson.

Hidden in the mix are the faceless others, who made their final trek by horse-drawn wagon, shrouded in evening fog, up the pasture behind the prison, to the cemetery. Above San Quentin State Prison, Marin County, California, sits Boot Hill, where unclaimed bodies lie, a place of forgetting.

Howard Hogan was sentenced to six to ten years in San Quentin—a name that grinds, grates, penetrates—notorious from the start for its stabbings and laundry-room sodomies, uprisings in a chaos of alliances, the ups and downs of who you are, who you know, and how that can help or hurt.

The prison's most striking feature has always been its unlikely location. Its imposing sickly yellow stone edifices, built shortly after the California gold rush, occupy a priceless piece of Marin County waterfront property, a gentle promontory jutting into the north side of San Francisco Bay.

The beachfront is slender, rocky, littered with spent jellyfish and washed-up kelp, serene if it were not just a spit and a curse away from the guard tower and the south-looking cell blocks, where the luckiest inmates could, if so moved, almost reach out and grab the fog that tumbled in, mush thick, through the Golden Gate and across the bay.

Drift to the realm of imagining and you might forget you were a prisoner. For a moment or an hour, you could lose yourself in the rhythmic slap of shallow waves licking the slender shore, the gulls and their cries, the maritime bustle, barges and boats passing your barred windows, jaunty freighters on their way to the Port of Oakland to unload before turning around and heading back out the gate.

You could witness, if you could dream, vistas and visions of a perfect kind of freedom.

South, one nautical mile.

West now, out toward the gate.

On to the raging Pacific.

Next stop, Shanghai.

◎

I like to imagine Howard Hogan was one of those whose cell faced south, that he could see the ships, the waves in dance. I imagine he heard a chorus of gulls picking at oysters, pecking, gulping, flying off to new promise, maybe a fishing vessel or a crossing ferry. If my grandfather's stories are true, that south-facing cell would have been where Howard Hogan read Sinclair Lewis, not once but many times. *Arrowsmith* was the book that inspired him to study medicine, to seek the true meaning of nature and healing, for others, for himself. He asked to work in the prison hospital.

A year into his sentence, the *Oakland Tribune* reported that Howard Hogan had been tapped to teach navigation to inmates in the prison's continuing-education school. Navigation. The art of getting from one place to another, usually by ship, *navis*. This without wrecking on shoals, underwater rock juttings, anything that might prevent you from getting from here to there. Navigation helps you find a safe way out, secure passage to the next port, maybe even to home.

Howard Hogan spent less than two years in San Quentin before his early parole for exemplary behavior. His release, the newspapers buzzed, was because of his family's wealth and influence. Probably. As far as my family knows, he never spoke to, never again heard from, the entertainer Al Jolson, whose fame and money grew in Hollywood's new "talking movies." No Jolson biography I could find mentions the night of June 1, 1924, when the singer abandoned his show and made a hasty getaway from Oakland, California. A month after that night, Jolson said it was his voice. Yet at the time he left a strange note for his manager, saying, "I'm through." Was Howard Hogan telling the truth about trying to save the lives of the two men smashed by his speeding car?

Howard left the country and earned his medical degree. He became an anesthesiologist, set up his own practice in Dallas, published in medical journals. The newspapers reported his marriage to a girl from Virginia. On the occasion of Howard Francis Hogan's death by cancer in 1948, age forty-eight, the Dallas County Medical Society approved a resolution honoring "this public-spirited man ... so that future generations may know and appreciate his splendid character."

In a Dallas medical journal, his obituary listed two pages of discoveries, his legions of offices, experts he had known, lives he had changed or saved, many more lives than two. The obit made no mention of the accident, of Howard's time in San Quentin, of his official pardon ten years after his release, a cleansing, erasing, of his early history.

My father always said that Howard's prison sentence was the best thing that could have happened to him, a gift, not a punishment. The whole episode in Howard's life, my father said, was transformative. A Japanese maple blooming. A human season turning. A fuller, more wholly conscious being emerging from the rubble, the same way people often describe near-death experiences, or war, or fierce winds altering landscapes and the people in them.

From the moment I first read about Howard Hogan in the yellowed newspaper clippings of the *Oakland Tribune*, I felt drawn to him, sensed a familial gift, that his story had something to teach me. I think I understand now. Howard's trial was a storm that swept through a life, downing the hat-racked banyans, the lesser trees, things that might have kept him from becoming what nature intended. I didn't know then either how or why, but

I wanted my life to change like that. And when the hurricane swept through our county, almost leveling our lives, I survived the trial. Something happened. My inner landscape transformed. The words came back.

My grandfather said he "cried like a baby" when his little brother Howard Hogan died, cried for the Hogan who found his way.

No one cried when Old Man Hugh died in an Oakland home for indigents, age ninety. No one mourned the lumber baron who sold his business and lost it all in the Crash of 1929.

Somehow, the Old Man evokes the poet Shelley's "Ozymandias," the once-towering titan whose wind-worn shrine in the desert called him "King of Kings," warning "Look on my Works, ye Mighty, and despair!" But after time and sandstorms, after the march of history, the eddies of generations, "Nothing beside remains. Round the decay / Of that colossal Wreck, boundless and bare."

My father never read Shelley's poem. But I know he would have loved it.

Sometimes I see the numbers in my mind, the growing numbers. Zero … One … One … Two … Three … Five. Then soon, 144. And on up. I wonder where my number fits in the pattern. This mathematical mystery, the Fibonacci sequence, was named after the thirteenth-century Italian mathematician who uncovered it. Start with zero and one, then each new number in the sequence is the sum of the two numbers before it. The true mystery in Fibonacci's numerical pattern is its occurrence throughout nature. It explains the spirals of the growth cycle, most notably, in the nautilus shell. The elegant shell, so perfect in form, is mathematically precise in its pattern of growth, suggesting, as my father once observed, ever-expanding creativity. The size of each successive chamber of the creature's spiraling home contains the sum of the two chambers before it. Fibonacci. In the theoretical world, science tells us, if a nautilus were to continue growing years and years past its natural cephalopodious life, the shell it left would first cover the barbecue pit, then an entire beach, then counties, then a continent.

As the shell grows, so have my thoughts about it. I am convinced that the pattern of the nautilus reflects how some humans learn, how they mature, as creators of texts and art and ideas, as people who live lives fully. Many artists, thinkers, actors, builders, even students, are like the nautilus, programmed to use what they see, do, and learn to build ever-larger chambers, pushing forward to the next, and the next, in boundless creation.

Other people, those who either cannot or who refuse to move forward, to grow, are clams. Nice clams, competent clams, maybe even big clams. But they will never push beyond the limits their shells impose. Why? Genetics? Personality? Intellect? Environment? Or just the unknowable will of nature, of the sea.

Howard Hogan emerged from calamity and a prison sentence into a life of researching, practicing medicine, saving lives. I can only imagine what chambers he would have filled had he not died so young. My grandfather Will, whose intelligence augured such promise, never could move beyond his desire to be a well-read gentleman of means and leisure. When that inheritance disappeared before his eyes, he snapped shut. He merely aged.

My father, everyman literary editor, was a nautilus many times over. I am sure, though, that he would not have said that about himself, would not have seen the accretion of knowledge, creativity, the understanding of what resides within, what the deepest eddies hold. He gardened. Shed tears if he stepped on a beetle. He was a lover of books and ideas, a student of the philosopher Martin Buber, among other thinkers. He was a journalist who walked among literary giants, reviewed them, conversed with them, sometimes even discovered them, and who had their thanks. I believe he lived in awe of the size of the chamber he had created, was sure he could never fill it, but then filled it anyway, and grew still-larger ones.

When he was in his seventies, years after his career at the paper, he discovered an art school tucked high in the redwoods of our hometown. He called the teacher there his "guru." Her gift was tapping into currents of genius residing in unlikely places. Like the rumpled figure of my father, dandruff on his sweater vest, walking with a cane now, dark-rimmed glasses flecked with snow dust sliding down his nose, the crooked half smile making you wonder if he were in pain, deep thought, or both.

One day the art teacher asked, "Who was the first surrealist?" My father said: "God."

He escaped those last years into sketches and paintings, oil, pastel, graphite, watercolor, each one an experiment, wild seascapes and ships, riots of color, splashes of cities with rain-blown street scenes. He had several art shows, but refused to sell any paintings. If someone admired a piece, wanted to buy it, he gave it away, a gift of thanks. In his notebooks, he painted the quirky, the grotesque, faces of ancient saints and early popes, hobos and merchants; towns and rivers and shoals remembered, blues and purples, bright as he remembered.

I can see him sitting out in his backyard studio reading about Klee, Pissarro, John Marin, Chagall, "my great enthusiasms," hunching over one of his creations, pastels in hand, glass of white wine always nearby. The man who had written enough to fill a shelf of books, suddenly painting, so fully engaged, a nautilus reveling in the glory, the expanse of its final chamber. A mind unleashed, bramble patches of imagination. Sweeps of earth and water and coastal towns; containers of souls, gods, and gardens. A twig with a lone blossom. A finely considered fern.

My own nautilus journey began in tight, small chambers, with a need to fill in brackets, to write into empty spaces, trying to make my story, the lives inhabiting it, whole. As those smaller stories grew larger, I have been able to piece together who my father was. I have tried to find those parts of him that reside in me still; to feel the blood rolling through us all. In some larger way, we are all, through accretion, the sum of those who came before us; of that which was once familiar, safe, moving into something new, unexpected, a larger chamber, each day a creative risk, the brackets mostly filled, a new page.

Soon after the hurricane, an envelope arrived with a check for $4,000. The money came from my great-uncle Howard's widow, Aunt Sally. When Sally died, she left a trust whose occasional beneficiaries included my father, Howard's favorite nephew. Since my father was gone, that final gift, ever strange, fell to my brother and me.

Happiness

FROM THE FINAL ENTRY IN MY FATHER'S NOTEBOOKS

Happiness, in the end, is the yes of things. A pretty good piece of art work at the age of 76. The smell of pastel and oil. A real place seen called Medjez el Bab. It was the day of ships and the ocean was always the Pacific . . . Quiet and thoughtful hours in his own backyard . . . The prospect of Mary Ann's return . . . Phyllis's hand clasp in the middle of the night . . .

So Long.

Watch Them Go

A nice Quote from Jan de Hartog, the Dutch-born writer, in a small book, A Sailor's Life: "For who are you, to think that no ship will sail any more after you are gone? Yet there is something in the thought that, however slightly, it is due to you that they are still sailing. So, to achieve that happy state of complete fulfillment, go to the cliffs, sit down and watch them go, for there goes your immortality."

My father would have loved that story. *Pennies from Heaven. Imagine!* I can hear him say it. And I know that, for a moment, he would be truly happy, enchanted with the quirky, epochal symmetry of it all, the way it all turns out, the time, the place, and the girl.

And right now, more than anything, I wish I could tell him that story, wish he could hear it, paint it in his notebooks, just once, before that morning when what looked like a freighter crawled on the dawn and we scattered his ashes to sea.

AFTERLIFE

Mary Ann wanted one more chapter, to tell the story of coming home, coming to terms, living her life, hiking the mountain, writing, teaching, hosting dinner parties, drinking wine in front of the big brick fireplace.

But she was not here to write it.

My name is Eric Newton. I am Mary Ann's husband, father to our two sons, and house human to Joe-Joe the flat-coated retriever—roles best measured by strength, not length, but if we need a number, the Hogan-Newton partnership spanned five decades, my entire adult life and most of hers.

I am her editor and she is my writer. Always. As writing partners, we season our stories like salt and pepper. I'm structure and function. She's music. She's magic.

◎

Again and again, often when we were in bed, we edited this book.

She called it her life's work.

We pledged fealty to this final chapter—*"All Hail the Unwritten!"*

The last time we went over the manuscript, after we finished, she just looked at me. It was not the please-grab-a-towel look but the deep-blue-sky look.

And she said … nothing.

Not a word. No need.

She was dying. We both knew what she was asking.

I hugged her pages to my chest.

"You know I'll do it."

◎

Perhaps home is not a place
but simply an irrevocable condition.
—*James Baldwin,* Giovanni's Room, *1956*

On April 25, 2016, Mary Ann's silver Camry barreled down an unlikely yellow-brick road—the Richmond–San Rafael Bridge—a lurking, battleship-gray double-deck steel cantilever structure, its girders so spooky that as a baby William always stared at them, wide-eyed, chanting ...

"Dar Dars! Dar Dars! Dar Dars!"

... until we got to the other side.

Our son forever named that bridge for our family, bolting us to it, people to place, even though we never knew exactly what he meant.

On that day in that car, Mary Ann drove, and friend Linda recorded the moment on video.

L: "Where are we, Mary Ann?"

MA: "We're ... under the Dar Dars! ... Mount Tamalpais ... Joe-Joe, look! ... the MARIN COUNTY LINE!"

Both: "WHOOO! WHOOO!"

Delirium.

Windows down, volume up, Edward Sharpe and the Magnetic Zeros blasting out their song "Home."

Mount Tamalpais, the Sleeping Lady, relaxed under a watercolor sky, kissing the clouds that run shadows over her forests, watching over Mary Ann's hometown.

As the silver Camry crossed the county line, Joe-Joe the dog shouldered his way into the narrow gap between the two front seats, like a roller-derby jammer, head on a swivel, trying to smell whatever was making these people scream.

Mary Ann, loudly: "WHOOOOOOOO!"

Joe-Joe felt the joy, strained in vain to lick the tears off her face.

Softly, she said, "Oh ... oh ... it's okay, Joe, it's okay."

No cargo hold for this excitable dog. Instead, we drove him

cross-country, Boca Raton, Florida, to Mill Valley, California, me at the wheel most of the way, Linda jumping in for the last lap, Mary Ann herself driving across the finish line.

Hello, Dar Dars and Western woodlands—*here we come!*

Goodbye, lymphoma (we thought) and Eastern swamp.

After twenty-two years away, using James Baldwin as her bridge, *there* is *here*, and *here* is *there*, and Mary Ann Hogan was home.

◎

In the days and months after she crossed the bridge, we settled into our new lives in the family home in Mill Valley, the place she loved best on earth.

She had a tall, smart corner desk ready to go, procured in Florida to match her new life as an English professor. As a study, she claimed her old room.

Anchor-gray poles hold up the three-level orangewood contraption. The desk itself really was not *her*. But everything on it was (and is). Carefully curated from work and love, the desk was her page; the artifacts, her words.

On the top shelf: a foot-long, gold-leaf, ibis-headed Thoth, Egyptian god of scribes; four little Haitian voodoo dolls, feathery pinks and purples, one a fortune-teller, standing in a child-sculpted sage-colored clay cup; a pen and ink sketch of a Pisan in Palermo in World War II and a watercolor of three zany clowns, both by Bill Hogan; and a print of a typewriter with the Anaïs Nin quote: "We write to taste life twice." (Mary Ann touched the totem of Nin each time she sat down "to greet with tepid hope a new blank page.")

The middle shelf: a color photo of sons William and James at Rodeo Beach, her favorite; two larger sequined, ribboned voodoo dolls in gold and yellow; a red and gold glove-size cloisonné box, empty but still a story; a black bumper sticker with white western letters, saying MILLBILLY; a vintage fist-size floral box that opens into a tiny crèche, a complete tableau in three cubic inches, hand-painted, thumbnail-size people and animals, all looking good except for the ass, which as it witnesses the birth of baby Jesus, looks something like a kangaroo.

The desktop: a cheap Dell computer, jumbled story notes, and the coolest thing of all—hanging down from the middle shelf, a mobile, a piece of floating whimsy just where a writer might look when lost in thought.

The mobile's distressed wire and beach-colored beads twist down to a crazy fluorescent, harlequin-green sign, under that a tiny, weathered cowbell, a bell that jingles just like the one in the movie we watched every Christmas, *It's a Wonderful Life*, little Zuzu saying, "Look, Daddy. Teacher says every time a bell rings, an angel gets his wings."

The mobile's crazy green sign says but one word: **Imagine**.

Imagine, as in the John Lennon song. A dreamer he was, and not the only one.

On a mild December evening in 1980, Lennon was shot four times in the back by a religious right-wing madman with an American-made revolver.

The *Oakland Tribune* mourned John Lennon on page one with a personal story by Mary Ann, then a young journalist. She evoked the spirit of the 1960s, said it would live on, still believed that decades later at her telltale desk with the harlequin-green mobile and the tiny, weathered bell that rings when angels get their wings.

Imagine that.

Mary Ann's end game was *Shelf Life,* a piece of writing that "eddies into infinity." An unreasonable goal, perhaps. Yet her childhood home held a thousand silent witnesses to *Shelf Life*— a book for each square foot of house.

The library was tended by Bill Hogan, literary editor, whom Mary Ann called

the greatest of all influences in my creative life, my father, with his built-in redwood bookcases in every room in our tiny house, cases filled with names and titles I memor- ized as a child ...

I can still see the olive greens, browns, the faded reds of the dust jackets, some torn but never removed; no meaningful order ... I read in and around most of them, was read to from their pages.

It seeped in. And this is where a writer's, or at least this writer's, true influence begins— with the ether, the streaming ethereal power of those early surroundings ...

Part of me, I know now, writes because of the ether.

Mary Ann's writing students called her "M.A." She shared this Walt Whitman line with everyone: "The powerful play goes on, and you may contribute a verse."

Once, as Robin Williams delivers it in *Dead Poets Society*, Mary Ann jumped up, laughing, saying "Shitski . . . ! My verse is due TOMORROW."

Deadlines, she made them and taught her students to make them. Later, I would be overwhelmed by how fast so many young writers, most from the Chips Quinn Scholars Program for Diversity in Journalism, sent tributes. Said journalist Tonya Alanez of the *Boston Globe*, "She was a gift and my guide. She taught me to connect the dots . . . to strike a chord . . . to write with heart."

◎

The events that led to this book were set in motion by a despicable relative of brown algae, *Phytophthora infestans*. In 1845, this blight blew like the wind through Ireland's main food crop. Over the next seven years, the Irish Potato Famine killed a million outright. Another million fled. In all, one in four people were simply *gone*, many of them tenant farmers, all under British rule.

Patrick Michael Hogan, great-great grandfather of Mary Ann Hogan, lived in Ennistymon in County Clare. There, they called the potato famine *an Drochshaol*, the Bad Life.

Long before Emma Lazarus wrote, "Send these, the homeless, tempest-tost to me, I lift my lamp beside the golden door!"; long before her poem, "The New Colossus," was inscribed on the Statue of Liberty; before all that, Patrick Michael Hogan escaped to New York.

The exact year, we don't know. But he worked as a stone mason. Married. A son, Hugh Hogan—the Old Man, the lumber baron, patriarch of this book—was born in 1853.

Without the potato famine, Patrick Michael might have stayed in Ireland. Then Old Man Hugh wouldn't make and lose a fortune. Grandpa Will wouldn't walk out on his family. Bill Hogan wouldn't feel forever less than, and Mary Ann wouldn't wonder what has swirled down the generations to her.

But the famine did happen. And as scientists in the field of epigenetics will tell you, that kind of trauma *can* be passed on to future generations, because people inherit more than DNA. Children of trauma can have greater anxiety and other mental-health conditions, greater body mass, diabetes, a reduction in number and size of offspring, and even cancer.

Mary Ann and I talked often about this. Does that happen in all families, she wondered? How do you escape it?

When times were bad back in Florida, when she could not write, she would bury her freckled face in a couch pillow, hiding but for one crazed pile of mahogany hair.

The big stereo speakers we'd lugged around for thirty years would play Irish protest music from The Wolfe Tones.

These were the low days, when the writer felt old and done; the book, forever undone.

Creative nadir.

"What's wrong, sweetie? Are your people in jail?"

"Eeyagh ... turn it up ... please ...?"

She was talking about "The Helicopter Song" by The Wolfe Tones, fastest-selling ever in Ireland, celebrated the brazen 1973 escape from Dublin's Mountjoy Prison. An Irish Republican army rebel hijacked a helicopter, landed in midafternoon in the prison exercise yard. The guards thought it was an inspection visit. Then three men jumped in. Up like a bird and away they flew.

Mary Ann's angst was existential. She was in her own prison, unable to write, trapped, she felt sometimes, with her father's fathers and theirs, and even with her whole country.

Celebrating the great escape from Mountjoy always helped.

After we broke free of Florida and, we kept thinking, cancer, she celebrated her joyous return by starting a weekly column in our small local paper, the *Marin Independent Journal.*

There's an idea from ancient Japan at work here, a philosophy that embraces imperfection. They call it *kintsugi.*

Say you drop a Portuguese plate. Instead of throwing it out, you glue it back together. And instead of hiding the cracks, you light them up with powdered gold.

The break becomes a respected part of an object's story of service, a very nice way to treat a ceramic bowl. And people, too.

Mary Ann wrote for her local newspaper to come full circle, to be a reporter where she had been half a century ago, to honor her tribe, to reintroduce herself, cracks and all— but mostly, to find the last lost fragments, stick them in place with words and illuminate them.

Kintsugi.

Just as she began to chronicle "the people and pulse" of her hometown, Mary Ann's lymphoma returned. She kept going, kept writing, emailing a friend:

> *I was writing a column about a conductor*
> *... and then my pink rose bush assaulted*
> *me with scents ... I started trimming off*
> *the spent roses and humming Beethoven's*
> *9th Chorale—the most beautiful IN THE*
> *MOMENT AIN'T LIFE GRAND moment*
> *I can remember ...*
>
> *But it's so hard, everything seems to be fear,*
> *anxiety, blood work, gaining weight ...*
> *there has to be a way to get to the moments,*
> *and to start stringing them like pearls ...*

Her first column, "The Saga of the Fork," described a giant silver fork that appeared in the woodsy foothills of Mount Tamalpais at a tricky fork in the road. The city of Mill Valley took it down. People objected. The city gave it back. And the fork landed on its old perch "not far from where novelist Jack Kerouac and Beat poet Gary Snyder once crashed for a summer, art following art, era following era."

She wrote often in her column about local artists, many of them natives who predated the tech wealth now dominating this place:

> *Beneath the tony Tesla-worn surface of*
> *this friendly yet oh-so-pricey town runs*
> *a deep cultural current ... touching on*
> *local identity, tribalism, newcomers,*

*and why so many natives have had to
leave the place they love. In Mill Valley,
like it or not, a local is a Millbilly. Some
see the term as disparaging. Others, a
badge of honor. Depends on who's talking.*

She loved being a Millbilly and writing of local life; of the world-famous Dipsea Race, "a happening" that runs over the mountain to the beach; of city benches, "a pleasure that's out-lived free parking"; and even of spring, "that ineffable impulse to burst forth, spread a wing, a kind word, a good deed, to riot-ously bloom, in spite of it all."

On social media she wrote of "fog in the face at the dog park, the variegated smells my dog never experienced … which make him waggle…. People don't waggle in Florida. Neither do dogs." She posted a photo of her and Joe-Joe the flat-coated retriever at Bayfront Park. The caption was just one word: "HAPPY."

Mary Ann found column items everywhere. In the weekly messages outside the Mount Tamalpais United Methodist Church: "Don't put a period where God has put a comma." Or in a sign at the roadside produce stand: "Peace, Love and Pickles."

She hadn't written regularly for newspapers for decades. Her column won a state press award, and her mailbox filled with praise. *Kintsugi.*

Only her editor, close friends, and family knew of her secret. The cancer was back. Only when she could no longer walk did the column end.

◎

Odds were, she wouldn't get this disease in the first place: just one in fifty women in this country get non-Hodgkin's lymphoma. Odds were, my wife's lymphoma wouldn't mutate into its deadliest form. Only one in twenty do. After that happens, until recently, there wasn't much anyone could do.

Sick, weak, and in pain, a backpack of prescription poison dripping into her, Mary Ann grew tired of the odds, so irrelevant in their precision, averages of a herd when what matters is the individual.

She emailed this to herself:

> *A fireball. I have made the decision to not listen to or be affected negatively by all the studies that say I am a certain candidate for death; how the prognosis for this particular disease is not very heartening; how 80 to 90 percent of those who get a clear cancer-free scan at the end of treatment relapse within the year and it's downhill from there ... I have decided that for everyone who sits in any of those studies there are a few of us who weren't studied and who overcome because we ain't done yet and that is me. So effing there!!!!!!*

🌀

It started in Florida in the summer of 2014. Mary Ann felt a lump on her neck. We were at a wedding. "Do you feel something right here?"

Tests revealed "lazy lymphoma," a non-Hodgkin's strain, more formally called follicular lymphoma, a cancer of the white blood cells. "If you are going to have cancer," the Florida doctor said, "this is the one to have." It can just hang around, not grow, not kill.

She got "chemo lite." It hardened her veins, but her hair remained. By the following spring, her scan was "nice and clear." No cancer.

Our house took a year to prep and sell, then the silver Camry headed home.

Her vacation from disease lasted about eighteen months. Lazy lymphoma can return but then go dormant. So we watched and waited. By the summer of 2018, four years after the first lumpy lymph node, the cancer was growing again, changing into something called diffuse large B-cell lymphoma—"fast-moving bandits," Mary Ann called them.

That's when she got the 24/7 backpack of poison—five months of "high-dose" chemo. She had me shave her head before it took her hair.

◎

nadir | na·dir / nādər, nādir (*n.*):

1. the lowest point in the fortunes of a person or organization

Once a week during big chemo, when she hit bottom, the nadir, she needed a blood transfusion or a white cell booster to live. Nadir focused us on basics. *First things first. Take it easy. One day at a time.*

Simple yet elusive. "To affect the quality of the day," wrote Henry David Thoreau, "that is the highest of arts."

Even with good Marin County cancer doctors, "chemo heavy" was a fail. Despite all those months of "stumbling anemia," the disease had grown and mutated again, this time into the deadly double-hit lymphoma.

They don't really know why.

◎

We filled three "cancer books," soft brown faux-leather journals full as a pelican's beak with facts, flowcharts, feelings, plans, jokes, the exigencies of life ... "put some pumpkin in Joe-Joe's dog food tonight."

Finish this book about her father? Not now.

Mary Ann was a light-hearted patient, laughed easily, enjoyed being around people who saved lives. Always a journalist, she was bored by routine, fortified by crisis—and funny.

When a nurse asked what kind of birth control she was on, Mary Ann answered with a wry smile, "Antiquity!"

Once she awoke at 3:00 a.m. to announce: "There's not going to be enough parking for my memorial!"

"That's funny," I said, "you should write about that in the morning ... or do you plan to die tonight?"

"I am not threatening to die," she said. "I am just keeping my options open."

We talked parking.

◎

We went to San Francisco to try the new immunotherapy treatment, CAR-T, a pioneering therapy that reprograms T cells to kill the cancerous B cells.

There were risks. When her own immune system killed lymphoma, something called cytokines were released. Too much, too fast, and you get cytokine release syndrome (CRS). One in five times it causes brain damage or death.

It was the middle of the night when Mary Ann got CRS. She could not say her name. She could not say where she was. Tried to text but all that came out was "batch troll rut." They brought her back with steroids. That was the only choice, and it weakened the cure.

Still, in the spring of 2019, her first scan looked clean.

We dared to make plans, buy tickets to baseball, opera, Muir Woods. We talked about seeing the play *Hamilton* and going to her goddaughter's wedding in Montana. We started working again on this book, marveling that she would owe her life to, of all things, fragments, the microscopic proteins ringing her altered T cells, allowing them to see the lymphoma, to see it so they could kill it.

Odds were seven in ten that Mary Ann's second scan, in May, would be clean.

It was not.

The night before we were to see the doctor, a nurse sent me the scan. "You better look at this," she said. I looked. The cancer was everywhere.

Another man might have woken her to tell her she was going to die. I am not that man. I was numb, heartsick. But I was also the Guardian of Days. Today had been a good day. Tomorrow, when the family reviewed the scan with the doctor, would not be.

We would do this tomorrow.

I cried, scribbled questions for doctors, fell into bed, squeezed her warm, sleeping hand, told her how much I loved her, cried.

Am I a coward? Or is this how we live on Walden Pond?

"Inevitable demise," she later told friends. "Emotional whiplash," one said—and it was. One day, Mary Ann seemed cured. Then, suddenly, she had three weeks to live.

The doctors who told her said they were surprised.

To the young doc who was the first to tell us, of all the things to say, she replied, "This must be the hardest part of your job ..."

The bigger question, Mary Ann always taught, is not what but *why*. She gave students little gray river rocks etched with the word *why*. She quoted Ernest Hemingway, who left newspapers, as we did, because of that three-letter word—regular newspaper work, Hemingway said, is "who broke into what? Where? When? How? But never *why*, not really *why*."

"*Why*," she said, "pricks the heart of curiosity."

We never learned *why* her cancer came, *why* it turned deadly, or *why* the treatments failed. The doctors knew so much, but never *why*, not really *why*.

Our medical team had one last idea, an expensive drug, Revlimid. It might wake up her T cells. They said it's a Hail Mary. We called it the Prayer Pill. Every morning when she took it, we held hands and prayed.

God grant me the serenity
To accept the things I cannot change
The courage to change the things I can
And the wisdom to know the difference.

On the table on her side of the bed was a happy red Maranta, a rhizomatous perennial whose opal leaves sit flat in the day but rise up at night, leaves coming together, just in time for vespers. It's called the prayer plant.

"What is prayer?" she wrote in a letter to a friend. "Is it talking to someone? Is it finding a placid place within yourself? Is it about lifting your thoughts up to the forces of the universe?"

The doctor gave Revlimid a one-in-three chance.

Mary Ann grinned.

"Then I'll give you two-thirds of a goodbye, just in case the next time you see me, I'm dead."

Just over the hill from Mill Valley in the Muir Woods National Monument awaits a cathedral of ancient trees. The redwoods there date back two thousand years, when only the Coast Miwok walked here—*lightly, apologizing to any spirits they disturbed*—while on the other side of the world, the Roman Empire was falling, not at all lightly. A week before she died, I wheeled Mary Ann down the boardwalk to see the trees that live through history.

She was beautiful in a floral headscarf of blacks, pinks, and greens, big gold-colored African disc earrings, her eyes twinkling blue. We stopped at our "Partner Tree." At first glance, this redwood seems bigger than the others. Look up, though, and you see two towering trees sharing one massive trunk.

"Tell them we grew together," she said. "Rebuilt each other from the ground up until we did not know where one ended and the other began."

Redwoods—*Sequoia sempervirens*, the world's tallest trees—can reach up to 325 feet. The coast's banshee winds can't knock them down because redwood roots, though only six feet deep, reach out sideways more than a hundred feet, each root knit into others, binding tree to tree, trunk to earth, in secret primeval embrace.

A redwood, like Florida's banyan, is a God tree. When one falls, its roots spring up new redwoods, growing tall in a tight family circle around the missing mother, pushing up with what she gave them to touch the sky.

Our sons, both artists, work in technology and psychology. Mary Ann wanted them to read Ecclesiastes 3:1–8 at her memorial.

One day, William was practicing with her: "A time to be born, and a time to die ... A time to break down, and a time to build up ... A time to weep, and a time to laugh ... A time to mourn, and a time to dance."

"When we get to the word *dance*," William told me, "she grabs my arm and says, 'This part is important, I want you to remember it.'"

When she was a teenager, his mom said, she always went to the beach on the summer solstice with guitars and friends to build a bonfire and play and dance.

A week after Mary Ann left us, hundreds of young people gathered on Ocean Beach in San Francisco, on the summer solstice—our sons and their friends, with blankets, drink coolers, pizza makers, a drone, and a fire twirler. I watched with her sister, Michele Liapes, as they placed flowers in a pile the size of a bonfire around a picture of Mary Ann and her boys.

William and James were the DJs. They played their own music to the setting solstice sun.

A time to mourn, and a time to dance.

This part is important. Some things you give your children knowingly; other things, they just get.

Remember poor Old Man Hugh, the patriarch, lumber baron buried penniless in ground that had forgotten him, no silver dollars to jangle in the church collection plate.

What do you suppose the Old Man said when St. Peter asked: "Did they dance on the beach for you?"

Journalists often do their best work when people die. Between us, Mary Ann and I wrote or edited obituaries for parents, aunts, uncles, friends, children of friends, and ourselves.

Mary Ann hated "thing" obits. More than once, she said:

> *A lot of obituaries are essentially lies,*
> *beefed up resumes, and the secret stuff of*
> *who someone really is gets lost.... the lie*
> *is the list of achievements ... thing, thing,*
> *thing, thing ... as if that's what makes a*
> *person whole.*

She studied the gay community's press in the 1980s during the AIDS pandemic. The *Bay Area Reporter* printed obits written by friends, lovers, family. They told "who someone really is." In the mainstream press at the time, the dead weren't gay.

They didn't die of AIDS. They died in formulaic obits, in alphabetical order.

Before we married, she was a reporter at the *Oakland Tribune,* and I was the city editor. One day, she called me in tears. Our friend's teenage daughter was dead. Car accident.

"I am doing the obituary," Mary Ann said.

There's no room on the obit page for it, I told her. "We can't even get in the famous people."

The telephone went dead.

A few hours later, I heard space on the front page was being held for Mary Ann Hogan, the *Tribune* reporter known for her personal journalism. You see, the top editors told me, more teens are dying in car accidents, unnoticed by media. And it just happened in Oakland.

Her story was stripped across the top of the front page and retold by newspapers, radio, and television newscasts all over the state.

"We're putting a little life into it," Mary Ann said about her own obituary, which she was writing with her friend Kathy.

We would send it out on June 13, 2019, the day she left us. Excerpts:

> *Mary Ann Hogan, longtime journalist and*
> *beloved writing teacher, crossed over Thursday*
> *in the Mill Valley home she cherished, after a*
> *year-long tango with a rare form of lymphoma.*
> *Her husband, her two sons, and her dog were*
> *with her. Mary Ann saw death not as an*
> *ending, but rather as the beginning of the final,*
> *infinite chamber in the nautilus shell of a*
> *creative life....*

*Mary Ann pushed the boundaries of teaching,
writing, cooking, singing, gardening, living—
whatever she took on. She raised a family
and made friends with the same artistic
passion. . . .*

*Her stories explored the human condition, with
headlines such as: "Why We Harp and Carp"
or "Twigged Out: The Nesting Instinct." . . .*

*One day, Mary Ann got a message from a nun
asking "Are you the author who wrote this story
about 'Why We Cry'? "If so, can you please
send me a new copy? I have been Xeroxing this
one for 10 years for my workshops for homeless
women—and can no longer read the type." . . .*

*Mary Ann sent the story—and then flew to
Southern California to lead one of the nun's
workshops . . . (with bags of clothes for the
homeless women).*

You get the idea. Mary Ann always was good at endings.
Me, not so much.

At first, losing her felt like losing both arms. You still feel
them there, still try to reach out, to touch, but you can't. They
are just gone. And every time this happened—and in the weeks
and years that would follow, it would happen all the time—there
would be this panicked silence, and then I could see it, the empty
space where the rest of me used to be, and on the bad days, I
would fall into it, into a soulless hole, my grief darker, deeper
still as I spun, out of control—until I couldn't think at all and
all I felt was sick.

The greater the love, they said, the greater the grief.

Though I lack the art
to decipher it,
no doubt the next chapter
in my book of transformations
is already written.
I am not done with my changes.
                     —Stanley Kunitz, "The Layers," 1978

Most people believe death is not The End. When Mary Ann called the afterlife the Great Mana Pool, she evoked "a big bonk of energy," cosmic background radiation, other dimensions and some sort of "divine Gatorade." Said she would leave on the Stardust Express. Her Earth suit, made of the ancient dust of stars, would return to stardust. The hospice chaplain called her the Queen of Stardust.

Like her mother, Phyllis, Mary Ann believed in the wisdom of all religions. Pick the best parts. Like the Polynesians believing the magic of mana can live in anything and, like karma, can be won or lost. Gain it with love, empathy, respect. Gain it by writing stories, creating music and art.

"Anyone can be a consumer," she always said. "Be a producer."

Mary Ann wanted to end where she began, in her childhood redwood home, in her bed, in her room, in the little Circle Way house on the hill behind the high school.

Five miracles made her wish come true.

The first: A top nurse in midnight-blue scrubs urged us to join hospice. We trusted her as if she had sung at our wedding, since she had. Our old friend just happened to work in the cancer clinic.

The second: Mary Ann wanted her body to linger after she left it. We had no clue what to do. But one of her writing students just happened to work at the mortuary. So, no problem.

The third: Everyone longed to trade goodbyes. It was too late. Mary Ann asked for quiet. A friend, Sarah, emailed her request. It was as if a giant switch had been thrown in the neighborhood. Roofers stopped roofing—mechanics, tree trimmers, even barking dogs—all noise just stopped. It was so still you could hear the light shine.

The fourth: Mary Ann wanted me, our sons, and Joe-Joe by her side at the moment she crossed over— three men and a dog (four men to her). Fed through the kindness of our friends and neighbors, we sat. Her in a vermillion scarf, smelling of China Rain and musky black dog, we sat.

When she let go her last breath, we fell out of time, sobbing forever, together.

The last: At the end, a miracle death is the one that comes in peace and with love, the biggest wonder of all, now as it was then, when Mary Ann's mother died just so, in the same room in the same little house on the hill behind the high school.

Partway up Mount Tamalpais, at the O'Hanlon Center for the Arts, where Bill Hogan took art classes and showed his paintings, I read the story of the five miracles to Mary Ann's fellow artists, her tribe.

After, our son James took the wheel of the silver Camry and drove home to Hogan House on Circle Way—the "house that cradled me," she wrote—where babies have been and will be christened, and family dinners welcome all.

Everything comes back to Circle Way, to the way of things.

The nautilus shell curling, wild geese flying, rain forests springing to life after hurricanes. Countries coming back after pandemics. Potatoes that die, redwoods that don't. Life and death and life. Books written and read, or not. Cycles broken, new ones created. Or not.

I remember visiting the Circle Way cul-de-sac more than forty years ago for my first Hogan family dinner. It was the summer of 1979, the evening chill no match for the roaring fire tended by Bill Hogan, who looked every bit the "sweet, sensitive, lugubrious Irish soul" of his daughter's description.

Stories poured like wine. I couldn't get enough. I was the managing editor of the local weekly newspaper, the *Mill Valley Record*, just twenty-one and enthralled as Steinbeck and Baldwin looked down from the old redwood bookshelves and the Hogan family discussed the issues of the day.

Bill sat by the fire—a real big-time daily newspaperman!— and came unstuck in time, like Billy Pilgrim in *Slaughterhouse-Five*, his stories bouncing around from World War II to books and big ideas.

Everyone got in on it. Mary Ann helped finish one of her father's stories; I helped finish one of hers, and so it went. No matter what, the literary cargo always made it to port.

Each dawn since the night I met the Hogans has been a new swirl, a new world, a chance, as Mary Ann would say, to conjure everyday magic, "the way a ribbon turns a box into a gift." The magic is what brings the days of dancing on this green earth, of accidental beauty, the quality days when you find and honor the missing pieces and add your verse to Whitman's infinite play.

Circle Way, the street, is the place where neighbors started to meet weekly to cope with the COVID-19 crisis and then never stopped meeting. Circle Way, the state of mind, is the vibe that compels us to help each other.

We begin to end, and then end to begin again.

Sometimes, I sit in Bill Hogan's studio with his photo and his paintings, and I write and wonder. *What if life is just an intermission?*

Tomorrow, I could spend another day staring at the empty space where the rest of me used to be, maybe fall into it.

But what I will do, on Muir Beach with Joe-Joe the dog, in the morning fog, the mother fog, is hook driftwood.

Because that is the Yes of Things.

AUTHOR'S ACKNOWLEDGMENTS

I am indebted to many people for their generous reading and commenting on numerous versions of this book. In particular, I thank my writing partners Erin Hobbie and Roger Druin for their support and insight during the early stages; thanks to Michelle Hasler Martinez, without whose unwavering friendship, literary acumen, and tail kicks this manuscript would not be what it is.

A thousand thanks to my husband, Eric Newton, for his gifted editing, to dear friends Sarah Pollock and Tim Porter for their insights, and to Kathleen Lowenthal and Linda Davis Newgard for being there, always.

Most grateful acknowledgment goes to those professors at Florida Atlantic University who have inspired me in so many ways along the path: Mark Scroggins, Susan Mitchell, and Adam Bradford. Above all, there are simply no words to express my gratitude and appreciation for my mentor and guiding light, Professor Kate Schmitt, who believed in this project from day one, and who gave me the heart to keep going.

EDITOR'S ACKNOWLEDGMENTS

Gratitude beyond words for the support of sons William and James, and niece Annika, and friends Sarah Pollock and Tim Porter (again), Patricia Kabick, Katherine Rowlands, Mimi Johnson, Hilde Hartnett, Harriet Swift, Eve Messinger, Michele Liapes, Dennis Hogan, Thomas Hogan, Julianne Bice, Nina Gomez, Lorrie Gaylen Urmanita, Tonya Alanez, Megan Eisemann, Atlantis Beckham, and the late Dr. Sharon Melnick.

A special acknowledgment to Alberto Ibargüen, CEO and president of the John S. and James L. Knight Foundation; and Chris Callahan, former dean at Arizona State University, as well as to all who gave to the Hogan-Newton Fund for young journalists at the Miami Foundation. Heartfelt thanks to the hundreds of former students and colleagues from the Chips Quinn Scholars Program for Diversity in Journalism for their outpouring of appreciation for Mary Ann's teachings.

In Mill Valley, California, we are most grateful to the O'Hanlon Center for the Arts, where Bill Hogan learned to paint, to The Image Flow, which scanned his art, and most of all, to our compassionate neighbors here on Circle Way.

Excerpts from this book won literary awards from Zone 3 Press, the *Memoir (and)* literary journal, and *Coastlines* literary magazine. The author's proceeds from this book will support young journalists through the nonprofit Hogan-Newton Fund at the Miami Foundation.

SELECTED CITATIONS

Carson, Anne. *If Not, Winter: Fragments of Sappho*. New York: Vintage, 2003. Print.

Cavafy, C.P. "Waiting for the Barbarians." *Collected Poems of C.P. Cavafy*. Trans. Edmund Keeley and Philip Sherrard. Princeton: Princeton University Press, 1992. Print.

D'Agata, John. *The Lost Origins of the Essay*. Saint Paul: Graywolf Press, 2009. Print.

Darrow, Clarence. "Closing Argument, The State of Illinois v. Nathan Leopold & Richard Loeb, Delivered by Clarence Darrow." *Famous Trials by Douglas O. Linder*. University of Missouri–Kansas City (UMKC) School of Law, 1995–2011. Web. 6 June 2012.

Didion, Joan. "At the Dam." *The White Album*. New York: Noonday, 1979. Print.

Didion, Joan. *Slouching Towards Bethlehem*. Middlesex: Penguin, 1974. Print.

Dillard, Annie. *The Writing Life*. New York: Harper & Row, 1989. Print.

Dos Passos, John. *U.S.A.* New York: Modern Library, 1930. Print.

Eakin, Paul John. *How Our Lives Become Stories*. Ithaca: Cornell University Press, 1999. Print.

Frost, Robert. "Never Again Would Bird's Song Be the Same." *PoemHunter.com*. PoemHunter.com, 2013. Web. 19 Dec 2012.

Gornick, Vivian. *The Situation and the Story*. New York: Farrar, 2002. Print.

Hartsock, John. *History of American Literary Journalism*. Boston: University of Massachusetts Press, 2000. Print.

Hogan, Mary Ann. "Peniel (Ithica)," *Memoir (and)*, Sausalito: Memoir Journal, 2010. Print. p. 25–42.

Hogan, Mary Ann. *The Hurricane Notebooks*. MA thesis. Florida Atlantic University, 2013. Print—Journal. MS.

"Hurricane." *Merriam-Webster Online*. Merriam-Webster, Incorporated, 2013. Web. 10 Sept. 2012.

Keats, John. "On First Looking into Chapman's Homer." *Poets.org*. Academy of American Poets, 1997–2013. Web. 2 Jan 2013.

Lopate, Phillip. "Writing Personal Essays: On the Necessity of Turning Oneself into a Character." *Writing Creative Nonfiction*. Ed. Carolyn Forche and Philip Gerard. Cincinnati: Story Press, 2001. Print.

Marvell, Andrew. "The Garden." *PoetryFoundation.org*. Poetry Foundation, 2013. Web. 13 May 2012.

May, Rollo. *The Courage to Create*. New York: Norton, 1975. Print.

McPhee, John. *In Suspect Terrain*. New York: Noonday Press, 1982. Print.

Miller, Brenda. "A Braided Heart: Shaping the Lyric Essay." *Writing Creative Nonfiction*. Ed. Carolyn Forche and Philip Gerard. Cincinnati: Story Press, 2001. Print. p. 163.

Milne, A.A. "Disobedience." *When We Were Very Young*. New York: Dutton, 1943. Print.

Newton, Eric, ed., *Crusaders, Scoundrels, Journalists: The Newseum's Most Intriguing Newspeople*. New York: Times Books, 1999. Print.

Shelley, P.B. "Ozymandias." *PoetryFoundation.org*. Poetry Foundation, 2013. Web. 6 May 2012.

Sims, Norman. *The Literary Journalists*. New York: Ballantine, 1984. Print.

Yagoda, Ben. *Memoir: A History*. New York: Riverhead Books, 2009. Print.

INDEX

A NOTE ON THE TYPE

This book was set in Chronicle, a typeface designed by Jonathan Hoefler of Hoefler&Co in New York in 2002. Chronicle is a serif font classified as Scotch, a style that originated in Scotland at the end of the eighteenth century and was later popularized in the United States. Chronicle is known as a transitional design and combines the warmth of old-style typefaces with the precision of more modern ones.

Jonathan Hoefler is a two-time honoree of the National Design Awards and the only person to have received both the Prix Charles Peignot, the prize for typographic excellence awarded by the Association Typographique Internationale, and the AIGA, the design profession's highest honor. He is the subject of an Emmy-nominated episode of the Netflix documentary series *Abstract: The Art of Design,* and his work is in the permanent collections of both the Smithsonian Institution and the Museum of Modern Art in New York.

⌃ Mary Ann Hogan hiking Mount Tamalpais, 1986, photograph by Eric Newton

ABOUT THE AUTHOR

Mary Ann Hogan was an award-winning journalist and teacher whose credits included the *New York Times*, the *Washington Post*, the *San Francisco Chronicle*, and *Mother Jones* magazine. As a staff writer at the *Oakland Tribune*, she specialized in personal essays and for six years was syndicated nationally by the *Los Angeles Times*.

Hogan was the primary writer of the book *Crusaders, Scoundrels, Journalists: The Newseum's Most Intriguing Newspeople*. She trained Chips Quinn Scholars in the nation's top program for college-aged journalists of color; and she coached the *South Florida Sun-Sentinel* newsroom, working with journalists who went on to win the Pulitzer Prize for Public Service.

She lectured on writing through the American Press Institute and the Poynter Institute for Media Studies; and taught writing at San Francisco State University, Palm Beach State College, and Florida Atlantic University, where she earned a master of fine arts in creative nonfiction.

Returning to her childhood home in Mill Valley, she wrote a community column for the *Marin Independent Journal* before dying in 2019 of lymphoma. The Hogan-Newton Fund at the Miami Foundation makes gifts to young journalists in her name.

Running Sea